DATE DUE		
MAY - 8 2001			
NOV 1 8 2004			

Also by Ellie Wymard, Ph.D.

Divorced Women, New Lives

MEN
ON
DIVORCE

MEN
ON
DIVORCE

✠

Conversations with
Ex-Husbands

✠

Ellie Wymard, Ph.D.

Hay House, Inc.
Carson, CA

Copyright © 1994 by Ellie Wymard

Published and distributed in the United States by:
Hay House, Inc.
1154 E. Dominguez St.
P.O. Box 6204
Carson, California 90749-6204

Edited by: Jill Kramer
Typesetting/internal design by: Freedmen's Typesetting Organization,
   Los Angeles, CA

Library of Congress Cataloging-in-Publication Data

Wymard, Ellie
    Men on divorce : conversations with ex-husbands / Ellie Wymard.
        p.   cm.
    Includes bibliographical references (p.   ).
    ISBN 1-56170-096-7 (alk. paper) : $12.00
    1. Divorced men—Psychology.   2. Divorce—Psychological aspects.
3. Man-woman relationships.   I. Title.
HQ814.W96   1994
306.89—dc20   94-17584
                                                                            CIP

ISBN 1-56170-096-7

99 98 97 96 95   5 4 3 2 1
First Printing, August 1994

Printed in the United States of America
on recycled paper

For three men:
My sons, Josh and Peter,
and for Buddy, my husband

C O N T E N T S

WHILE WRITING my first book, *Divorced Women, New Lives*, I became aware of how little of the material on divorce focuses on the experiences of men. But when I talked about writing a companion book based on interviews with ex-husbands, women would respond with little variation: "Everyone knows *their* stories anyway." Similarly, males would scoff, "You'll never get men to open up."

Such negative remarks buoyed me to test the water. My chance came when a distinguished gentleman, leaning forward on his tweed elbow at a dinner party, caught my unsolicited attention and offered: "If you ever write a book on divorced men, I'd like to be interviewed. I consider myself to have been an abused man."

An appointment was arranged, and when we subsequently spoke in his suite of offices, I heard similarities between his description of oppression and that of the divorced women I had interviewed. For example, although he enjoyed an international reputation as a legal scholar and jurist, his wife demeaned his accomplishments, and this personal ridicule and rejection caused him deep humiliation. In contrast with his successful public image, the insecurity of his private self was surprising. It reminded me of the oft-heard complaint made by the educated wife with a professional career who is, nonetheless, treated like the "little woman" at home.

As my interviews continued, I became more gender blind. So many of the stories I heard were disturbing because they ran counter to common perceptions on how men experience marriage and deal with divorce. Not only had many men suffered terribly within their marriages, but also during the separation and divorce process. The disappointment, frustration, and loneliness that I watched them struggle to express were the same emotions that divorced women ached to remember, but seemed to verbalize with less strain. Unlike women, men locked away their stories of divorce in their hearts and minds, but once invited, poured out their words in a cathartic manner. In my conversations with more and more men, I discovered untapped wells of buried pain.

To explore the male side of divorce is not to betray documented evidence regarding the economic hardship and psychological stress that divorce places on ex-wives. Women and children are indeed the financial losers in divorce. But in an effort to support their cause, we have made divorce a single-sex issue. In comparison to the attention given to women and divorce, the experiences of former husbands have been neglected and minimized.

This neglect encourages the perception that men are callous to disappointment, hurt, and grief, and do not require nurturing even when going through one of life's worst personal crises. To borrow Shylock's words, we widen the gap that men are not "subject to the same diseases, healed by the same means, warmed and cooled by the same winter and summer" as women are. Far worse, we promote the view that marriages that go sour must be the husband's fault, and that the loss of wife and children means little to him. In general, we are blind to the problems of divorced men—unaware of the loneliness they endure, the confusion they feel, the situations they tolerate, the guilt they carry, the abuse they withstand, and the efforts they make to preserve their marriages.

Thirty years ago, the publication of Betty Friedan's *The Feminine Mystique* freed women to talk about themselves and identify with the lives of other females. They learned to trust each other in new ways through the sharing of personal stories. Their reading of essays, fiction, and poetry written by women further validated for them the ways in which women experience life. The fantasy of the "zipless fuck" in Erica Jong's *Fear of Flying* is an early example of women enjoying a mutual secret. But in a subsequent essay titled "Blood and Guts: The Tricky Problem of Being a Woman Writer in the Late Twentieth Century," Jong writes that it is time

> . . . to enter the next phase—the phase of empathy . . . We must consider ourselves free to explore the whole world of feeling in our writing—and not to be trapped forever in the phase of discovering buried anger . . .

Stronger even than anger is curiosity—emotional and intellectual curiosity—the vehicles through which we enter into other states of being, other lives . . . Exploration is a nobler calling than war.

Because the public's critique of divorce so suppresses the voices of men, *Men on Divorce* is an effort to break the silence, to allow men to explore the power of their own words so that we may "enter the phase of empathy." Their personal stories will sweep away assumptions about divorced men, exposing the turmoil, loneliness, emptiness, and despair that are human equalizers, no less the terrain of ex-husbands than ex-wives. Inviting men in from the sidelines to participate in the dialogue on divorce can be a step toward eliminating some of the factors that contribute to the break-up of one out of every two marriages in this country. Furthermore, it is reassuring for men in the process of divorce to know that others have experienced the same emotions, and have recovered.

Without question, the contradictions and tensions inherent in divorce are felt by men as well as women. Divorce is a human problem, not a segregated concern. *Men on Divorce* is intended to serve as a catalyst for adjusting the imbalance.

Ellie Wymard
Pittsburgh, PA

A C K N O W L E D G M E N T S

I am grateful for:

the encouragement of Dr. Grace Ann Geibel, R.S.M., President of Carlow College, Pittsburgh, Pennsylvania, who understood the time I needed to complete this book.

the trust of 45 men who told me their stories, but whom I cannot thank by name because of the privacy that they deserve.

the friends who recommended divorced men for me to interview.

the hours of professional time granted me by the following psychologists and psychotherapists: Dr. Bruce W. Barth, Dr. Ralph P. Brooks, Cathleen Fanslow-Brunjes, Eileen Colianni, Dr. A. Barbara Coyne, Roland P. Dorval, Dr. Douglas Gillette, Joseph Jastrab, Alice Kushner, Dr. Herbert I. Levit, Paul Lyons, Dr. Terrance O'Connor, Dr. Neil Rosenblum, Judith A. Talbert, Kimberly W. Underwood.

the knowledge I gained because of those willing to share their insights, research, and expert opinion: Bruce Burrows, Todd Erkel, Bob Frenier, Jack Gandy, Randy Genrich, Dolores Giauque, Jim Hanneken, Ed Honnold, Esq., Patricia Jameson, David L. Levy, Esq., Rose Palmer-Phelps, Carol Randolph, Chris Stafford, Irene Surmik, Janet C. Ziegler.

the generous legal advice of Judge Lawrence W. Kaplan and Attorneys Ronni K. Burrows, Norma Chase, Fredrick N. Frank, Lynne N. Krenney, Max A. Levine, James E. Mahood, Hilary A. Spatz, Joann Ross-Wilder, Ellin H. Wymard, Joseph M. Wymard.

the legal research provided enthusiastically by my son and daughter-in-law, attorneys Josh T. Wymard and Virginia Parker Wymard, and attorney Lauren MacVay.

the prompt responses of my researcher, Rose Ann Opferman.

the friends who referred me to therapists, and warmly supported my work in many different ways: Among them, Nancy Beck, Gerry and John Boccella, Jack Christin, Jane Coleman, June Delano, Mary Devlin, Marilyn Donnelly, Joan Dorgan, Mary Cay Hayden, Martina Jacobs, Margaret Kelso, Charlean Kratt, Mary Lou McLaughlin, Eileen Riddle, Barbara Seltman, David Stanko, Louise Wells, and the Friday Afternoon Faculty Reading Group at Carlow College; and most especially, Alyce Christin, who was here at the beginning. And Mary Ann Eckels, who stands alone.

the memory of Dan Olmos, the first editor for *Men on Divorce*, who offered guidance and hope.

the perceptive incisiveness of Jill Kramer, the editor who followed Dan with grace, and finished *Men on Divorce* with me.

the confidence of Josh and Peter, my two sons, whose "Hi, Mom, how's the book?" never failed to touch me.

the patient faith, bolstering humor, and sustaining love of Buddy, my husband.

"WHEN I FIRST SEPARATED from my wife, I was desperate to read anything I could get my hands on about divorce. But I couldn't find much, except in women's magazines. So I would read them in waiting rooms, or buy *McCall's* or *Vogue* at the newsstand. Then I had to turn myself upside down, trying to apply what I had read about women and divorce to my experience as a man."

It is hard to picture the former college baseball and basketball star who spoke these words thumbing through *Vogue* in search of a role model. But his experience is common among divorced men. The scarcity of material with which they can identify is one of the primary factors that contributed to men's willingness to be interviewed for this book.

For example, to prove his love for his wife, whom he thought objected to the demands of his career, a 42-year-old U.S. Army colonel resigned before he was to be promoted to the rank of brigadier general. Simultaneous with his separation from the army, he was served divorce papers—his wife was leaving him for another man. "I felt abandoned," he said simply, "but I couldn't find anything to read from a male perspective. I wanted to know if other men felt this way. The most balanced approaches to abandonment are written from a woman's perspective. But abandonment should be dealt with from either perspective. It's not just a female phenomenon."

The irony of this insight is that male experience has always been the stubborn standard for understanding female behavior. Historically, women have been treated, in the words of Simone de Beauvoir in her classic study *The Second Sex,* as "the Other." In all aspects of life, what it means to be a woman has been interpreted in terms of what it means to be a man. As a generic term, *man* seldom includes *woman.* Yet our basic comprehension of the dynamics of divorce is defined by the experience of wives and mothers, not husbands and fathers. Efforts to understand the emotional effects of divorce generally exclude men or relegate them to the invisible position of the "second sex."

"This sounds terribly maudlin, and I'm not sure why it is," apologized a physics professor, "but women are able to be more completely open about their emotions with other women than men are with each other. And women can find plenty of material in magazines to help them through divorce. Even *Reader's Digest*, for God's sake, carries some advice about the way women can work out this feeling or that. But there are hardly any men's magazines that talk about things deeper than football or carpentry or mechanics. There is still an American machismo that wants to ignore the more sensitive side of life."

My own ingrained assumptions about masculine behavior unraveled while interviewing men who cried while sitting behind their polished desks in sky-high offices when a question reminded them of lost love. In describing how divorce caused them to miss the daily happenings of family life, computer designers, attorneys, business executives, and engineers frequently acquired the poet's eye. Their tears made me recall Robert Frost's lines at the end of "Birches":

> . . . Earth's the right place for love;
> I don't know where it's likely to go better.

A civil engineer, for example, once handed me a picture from his bookshelf, and explained, "Material possessions can be regained, but I didn't get to see my daughter dressed for her first prom. That moment can never be recaptured." Divorced men feel most vulnerable when excluded from celebrating family milestones such as birthdays, annual picnics, or graduation ceremonies. "If the kids are in a play, and my ex-wife and I are off-stage to greet them, you wonder which one they will go to first." Memories of the public and private rituals of marriage press in upon ex-husbands, particularly when they are newly divorced. But those men who are childless are no less nostalgic about losing their domestic history.

A Washington lobbyist, married 15 years, described his loss: "There's a huge hole in my life right now. Life is a series of experiences which become memories with the passage of time. Divorce means that you lose the ability to reflect with someone on your past and about your future together, and how we grow and change and experience. My wife has the house, the travel pictures, the measuring cups in the kitchen. Possessions and memories are a part of personal identity. The hardest thing is knowing that I won't be able to look back on things we did together and what it was like to be there. Years are gone that can't be replaced."

Divorced men are not expected to speak in such a confessional way. But the 45 men interviewed for *Men on Divorce* admitted their shortcomings. Few were self-righteous, even when believing that their wives provoked the situations that escalated to the point where divorce was necessary. They represent various ages, careers, and economic levels. Each man's story of divorce is distinctive.

The range includes husbands who were blind (or chose to be blind) to their wives' infidelity, and husbands who were downright betrayed. Included are husbands who opposed the idea of their wives working outside the home, and husbands who reluctantly agreed to this arrangement. Other men wholeheartedly supported their wives' professional careers until the birth of children complicated the division of labor. A few are long-suffering husbands who coped with their wives' sustained illnesses. Some men were cruelly treated with physical and verbal abuse. Others admitted to having been wife-batterers.

A more sensational case is that of the corporate executive who finally invited his wife's female lover to live with them in a last-ditch attempt, he said, to have done "everything possible to eventually set things right again." Counter to the stereotype, husbands can assume the passive, trusting, optimistic behavior in marriage that we generally attribute to wives.

In an extended conversation, the men interviewed for *Men on Divorce* answered a series of questions that had not been given to them in advance of our meeting. The questions followed the sequence of their marriage and divorce:

1. How did you meet your wife?
2. When and why did you decide to marry?
3. How did your families feel about your marrying each other?
4. What were your expectations of marriage?
5. What was your lifestyle like with your wife?

6. Did you share the same interests and values?
7. Did you support each other's interests?
8. What were the high points of your marriage?
9. How did the problems start?
10. What were the problems?
11. When did you suspect that the marriage would not work?
12. What was the lowest point of the marriage?
13. How soon after that did you separate or divorce?
14. Did you want to save your marriage?
15. Why did you want to save it?
16. What did you do to save it?
17. Did you seek counseling, therapy, or analysis?
18. How did you feel as you went through the process of divorce?
19. Did you need emotional support?
20. If so, where did you go for help?
21. How did it feel to ask for help?
22. What was your process of renewal?
23. How do you feel now?
24. What is it like to be single?
25. What is the best part and the worst part of being single?
26. In retrospect, would you do anything differently?
27. What qualities do you value in a woman now?
28. Would you marry again?
29. What is your advice to other men who are going through divorce?
30. What is your relationship like with your children?
31. Was your financial situation changed by divorce?
32. How do you think friends ought to treat divorced men?
33. Why did you submit to this interview?

When one looks at these questions in this list-type format, it might be inferred that I was intent on steering the conversation in one particular direction. But in most cases, the questions merely provided a framework for discussion. I truly believe that a person owns his story and should not be manipulated in the way he chooses to tell it. In fact, the most revealing moments in these interviews occurred when a man eventually felt enough trust to take the lead. I savored the instant that he would break away from the questions, because then I was sure to hear what was distinctive about him. On his own, through nuance, gesture, and words, he would bring his marriage and divorce to life. It is these characteristic moments that I have tried to capture here.

At such times, men do not speak about the *idea* of divorce, but about their *feelings* about divorce. They are not trying to make a concept clearer, but simply to make their emotions more understood. They want to describe how it feels to lose a wife and children. They want to change the popular assumption that men court divorce, deserve divorce, and suffer few ill effects—except in the financial area, when their marriages end. They explain how they cope with estrangement, remorse, guilt, and failure. By recalling hurtful memories, they draw us into their pain and vulnerability.

For example, I interviewed a lawyer in his townhouse kitchen in Arlington, Virginia, as he cooked for his first dinner party since his divorce. We teetered on stools at a narrow counter, juggling cups of lukewarm tea, a temperamental tape recorder, batteries, notepads, canisters of flour, and a bundle of worn-out black *Les Pens*. Describing how well-intentioned friends offered insensitive advice when he first separated, he suddenly began to cry deeply sorrowful tears when recalling how a professor from law school unexpectedly said, "Anything I can do, you call me, and I will stop whatever I am doing and I will go and do it."

My surprise at his outburst troubled me. It made me realize that the paradigm of divorce is so rigidly fixed on the problems of women and children that the sight of a tearful man appears to be a radical distortion. Men have not been encouraged to claim the truths of what divorce does to them. Ultimately, this is a disservice to everyone. At best, ex-husbands are deprived of the support that comes from knowing that other men have shared their pain. Women are disadvantaged because the more men are treated as "the Other" in divorce, the more distant and mysterious their thinking remains. With this attitude, we risk stretching the difference between male and female needs into an inviolable separateness that no effort will be able to bridge. But until their voices are heard as well, ex-husbands will remain "the Other," a position that forces divorced men and women into opposite corners, as if nothing were to be gained if their stories would start to circle each other.

For example, husbands can suffer low self-esteem because of a wife's tyranny, a reversal of the stereotype generally applied to women. Regrettably, when husbands display their sensitivity, they are sometimes derided by wives who have stern opinions about masculine behavior. A skilled mechanic for an international airline was repeatedly called a wimp by his second wife for allowing his parents to remain friends with his first wife and their daughter. She wanted him to prohibit his parents from seeing their grandchild perform at school and church events.

He recalled, "I didn't think there was a need to make such a choice. I simply did not agree. The wimp factor got to the point that if I even rocked in my rocking chair, I was not being masculine. She called me a fag, and then wondered why I couldn't have sex with her. I said, 'You stop calling me these things,' because I enjoyed sex, and it was always important to me. I always had to prove myself to her by being hardboiled and confrontational. I'd make an ass out of myself arguing with my parents and friends. But I've been seeing another woman now for about six months, and I don't have to be afraid to be sensitive with her. When we saw *Field of Dreams*, we both cried, and I didn't feel self-conscious. When tears came down my face at my daughter's dance recital, she perfectly understood. I would have had to control myself with my former wife. Tears were not manly to her."

This honesty is typical of the 45 ex-husbands interviewed for *Men on Divorce*. They related their day-to-day struggles in trying to understand their marriages and in accepting themselves after divorce. Telling their stories was a way for them to shed the past and re-invent a life of new possibilities. As expected, each was at a different point of recovery, indicating renewal, confusion, or defensiveness. Some men wanted to communicate their suffering and anger; others sought expiation; still others wanted to convey how it is possible to deal affirmatively with divorce, accept responsibility, and commit to the future.

More importantly, the willingness of each man to talk about his divorce signals an acceptance that men can connect in new ways—

not by being tough, confident, and self-reliant, but by being open, questioning, and vulnerable. They related their stories in a conversational way so that other men would find consolation that they are not alone. In response, they hoped that these men in the cycle of divorce would begin their own individual journeys toward growth and transformation.

Thus, at the heart of this book is the belief that personal stories—in their telling and in their hearing—have the power to change lives. Part 1 of *Men On Divorce*, "Hurtful Memories: The Voices of Men," presents men's elliptical narratives with minimal commentary, so that readers have room to make their own connections and inferences. Issues surfacing from these narratives are explored in Part 2, "Who Am I Now? What Did It Mean? Where Am I Going?" Insights are provided by former husbands, therapists, counselors, and lawyers. Suggestions are offered for coping with grief, healing, and recovery. Practical advice is offered on how to choose a therapist, joining divorce support groups, knowing what to expect from friends, and understanding the realities of child custody.

The voices of men have been silenced on divorce as on no other complex human issue in our culture. If we truly want to understand and learn how they experience separation and divorce, we first need to turn to their own descriptions. Most men choose marriage as a way of finding personal fulfillment and happiness. Theirs is a human dream, not one that is the sole possession of young brides. But theirs is a story we have not really heard.

HURTFUL MEMORIES: THE VOICES OF MEN

BROKEN LIVES

He never found her, though he looked
*   Everywhere,*
And he asked at her mother's house
*   Was she there.*

Sudden and swift and light as that
*   The ties gave,*
And he learned of finalities
*   Besides the grave.*

from *The Hill Wife,* by Robert Frost

THE VARIOUS WAYS in which wives are deceived in marriage are more familiar to us than the betrayals that husbands endure. We presume that men are always in control of their own destinies. We do not expect them to be fooled. When they are, we rarely ask how they cope with loss. We think we know. Yet men who learn that their wives are engaged in sexual affairs feel hurt, humiliated, and rejected, as do women when the situation is reversed.

According to one recent study, only an 8 percent gap exists between husbands and wives admitting extramarital relationships. A 1993 survey of 1,400 people by the National Opinion Research Center at the University of Chicago concluded that 21 percent of men and nearly 13 percent of women admitted to having cheated on a spouse. The Kinsey Institute of Sex Research at Indiana University estimated in 1990 that 37 percent of married men and 20 percent of married women have been unfaithful.

Statistics on extramarital relations are hard to pin down, but the fact is clear that when their wives left them for other men, the ex-husbands whom I interviewed remembered feeling a terrible emptiness. They used images of death, illness, and physical debilitation to convey the

3 ✠

depth of their despair. Whether newly divorced or not, their scars were often fresh.

Chuck Schaefer, a 42-year-old retired U.S. Army colonel waiting for his divorce to become final, described his wife's infidelity and the divorce process as the most "gut-wrenching, terrifying thing I have ever gone through. I was in Vietnam and bailed out of airplanes. I saw my friends killed. I lived in the middle of death. I had polio as a child and was not supposed to be able to walk normally, let alone dream of joining the army. But this is the most painful of everything."

The distance of eight years had not helped Michael Coury, age 52, a successful environmental engineer, to forget how helpless he felt when his wife left him for a neighbor: "I felt as if I had had an amputation. I was nothing. Every day I woke up feeling that I had to die over and over again."

The despair that overcomes men who are betrayed can lead them to the brink of suicide. When Joe Petrak's wife left him at the beginning of December one year, he missed 9 out of 14 working days during the holiday season. Instead of reporting to his job as an airplane mechanic, Joe sat at home in a rocking chair. "I dwelled only on the good aspects of the marriage, not the bad," he sadly recalled. The rest of the time he tortured himself by circling around his wife's apartment to see if her lover was parked outside. Alone in the car, blinded by tears, Joe remembered thinking, "It would be so easy to go off the road and end it that way. The only thing that prevented me was the fact that my little girl wouldn't have a daddy anymore."

Husbands whose wives have secret affairs live in a domestic world created by lies and hypocrisy. They become desperate when recognizing the falsity of all they had once trusted. Ex-husbands who rescue themselves from hopelessness do so in a variety of ways, none of them miraculous. Moreover, the crucial issue of their wives' infidelity is more complex to them than the simple answer to the question, "Did she or didn't she?"

Post-Modern Split

Without a doubt, Stephen Marshall, a 35-year-old attorney, was a jilted husband. His wife, Ashley, who co-anchors the evening news for a network affiliate in the Southwest, left him for an electronic guitarist who plays on weekends in a hotel bar.

When Stephen met Ashley, she worked on the news desk for a television station in Chicago, where he was an assistant district attorney. They lived together for a year, and then had a "magic wedding. We were totally crazy about each other." Soon after their marriage, Stephen was happily situated with a major law firm, but Ashley felt frustrated that the station was not giving her enough time on the air.

Professional competition with Ashley was never an issue with Stephen, who "always thought that women should have the same career expectations as men. I was not about to assume the position that my career should have the attention and focus." Therefore, Stephen encouraged Ashley to send her résumés throughout the United States. When she landed a television talk show in Baltimore, Stephen submitted his resignation and followed her back East, where he was hired by a law firm in Annapolis.

But before too long, Ashley was unhappy again, bringing problems home from work every night. "I began to feel like a career counselor or a therapist," Stephen remarked, "but aside from that, we had a great marriage. We were the very best of friends. We never had a problem finding something to talk about. Ashley had a devastating sense of humor. We had a lot of fun together and a great sex life."

Stephen and Ashley had agreed to one more major move before establishing themselves permanently. But within two years, Ashley had an offer to co-anchor her own news show in the Southwest. "I loved my job; I was going to be made a partner in three months. We had just sunk a ton of money into remodeling a home," Stephen remembered, "but I got ready to move." For nine weeks, Stephen and Ashley had a commuter marriage, as he stayed back in Annapolis to sell the house and wrap up his cases. Although he was aware that Ashley was acting "weird and preoccupied," Stephen attributed these moods to the stress involved in their cross-country traveling.

The moving arrangements finally completed, Stephen could not wait to celebrate with Ashley. But on their first night together, she insisted on taking him to a hotel bar to meet a guitarist playing in a rock band. Eager to know what Stephen thought of him, Ashley revealed that they were lovers.

Stephen explained how he tried to be reasonable. "Ashley is an attractive blonde. She was somewhat of a celebrity in a new city, and we hadn't had a consistent relationship for three months. These things can happen. I felt we could work it out. So she had a fling, I thought. But only a few days had passed when she told me that she didn't want to have to make a choice between me and the rock guy. I couldn't accept that kind of selfishness. She was no longer someone I wanted to be married to and have as the mother of my kids. I was devastated that she waited until I had moved before springing all of this on me."

When Stephen told Ashley that he wanted a divorce, she disclosed that she was pregnant and did not know whether he or the guitarist was the father. Stephen left the decision up to Ashley about whether or not to have an abortion, and promised that if the child were his, he would offer economic support. But the baby would not cause him to stay married to her.

During his first week in a new job in a new city, and without one friend, Stephen dealt with the personal problems of infidelity, divorce, and abortion. He recalled wanting to "stay in bed forever and not wake up." To survive these critical days, he kept a journal, sought psychiatric help, talked daily with good friends in Maryland, and depended upon his family.

Stephen admitted, "I needed help. It wasn't a blow to my ego to reach out. I tried not to treat divorce as a failure on my part. I believe that a man gets himself together in a time of crisis by starting with what's inside him. I'm a problem solver, but that's not to say I'm a computer. Analytic skills come in handy during critical times, but I didn't cut myself off emotionally. I tried to ride with my feelings but not let them stand in the way of my decisions. Another person will not have a long-term effect on my will to live."

Stephen's journal-writing helped him uncover what he was experiencing on an unconscious level while he coped with the legal process of separation and divorce. He refused to become absorbed in the paperwork of divorce to the point of denying his personal turmoil. Putting down his thoughts in writing allowed him to be attentive to his feelings and watch the roundabout design of his healing.

Two years after his divorce, Stephen was still careful about forming serious ties with another woman. "Even now," he explained, "some memory will come into my mind, and the tears just roll. I know I can recover naturally, find happiness, if I don't rush things and screw it up."

Stephen's description fits the tightrope that ex-husbands find difficult to balance. It is the art of releasing their emotions while thinking clearly at the same time. They need to find safe outlets for expressing how they feel. Ex-husbands who are betrayed seldom develop a false faith in rationality, but when they are overwhelmed by grief, they worry about making confused judgments about their future.

Ashley's infidelity did not destroy Stephen's faith in marriage, though. He offered a poetic tribute to what he values: "I miss the intimacy of marriage. The routine, the secrets, the traditions that develop—the daily, mundane things that are a part of marriage, are what I love and miss. I saw us together at 60 years old. My dreams shattered, crashed overnight. And I raged with jealousy over my wife's having an affair."

Ex-husbands such as Stephen can be dealt very hard blows and still be wistful about what they once had. "If you are honest with yourself," Stephen insisted, "you never totally get over a person. Ashley had unique qualities that I loved and will never find in another woman. I will always miss her good points. Sometimes I still get angry, sometimes sentimental, but I let those feelings flow. I won't let them result in a decision that will affect my life."

In allowing himself to mourn the good times, Stephen paradoxically delivered himself from depression. He is not disillusioned about trusting and loving again.

Slipping Away from the Fifties

In 1964, 20 years before the wedding of Stephen and Ashley, Michael Coury, an environmental engineer, married Sally Bayard. The Courys' hopes for the future were no different from those of many young couples right before the rise of popular feminism. It was decided that Sally would teach high school history until becoming pregnant. At that time, to imagine that Sally would ever ask Michael to adjust his career goals in order to be more available to their growing family would have never occurred to them. After all, Michael's own father put in 16-hour days, and he, himself, had always expected to do the same. In time, Michael was working six straight days a week, including nights, and was frequently on construction sites for weeks before returning home.

Challenged by Sally to make a decision about his priorities, Michael changed engineering firms, took a pay cut, and worked more reasonable hours. "It was not a decision I made overnight," Michael admitted. "But Sally was alone with the children, and I realized that I wasn't much of a companion. My trips were never glamorous. Some days I would be in four cities and never see anything except airports and conference rooms. I was never unfaithful. My marriage was special to me. There was never anything I didn't like about Sally from the first day I met her."

Michael thought his marriage was stabilized, even though his career advanced at a slower pace than if he had not changed firms. For a number of years, Michael and Sally enjoyed simple pleasures together. She went to football games with him, and he attended poetry readings with her. "Maybe I was too tight-fisted," Michael worried after the fact. "Maybe I should have been more attentive, bought little gifts. But I would call and say, 'How about a date tomorrow night?'" At age 40, he and Sally had a baby girl.

Changes in Sally's behavior occurred slowly. She grew more and more disheveled, and she would disappear with the baby for the entire day, visiting museums and bookstores. The older children would not know where to find her after school and missed her during dinner. Michael left the office earlier and earlier. He assumed responsibilities for all the cooking, shopping, and parenting, except for care of the toddler, who roamed the city with Sally.

Although his wife's life became "completely unstructured," Michael could never confront Sally about the disruption in their family. Early in their marriage, he remembered that Sally lost her temper, and he was scared. "My mother and father loved each other, but they squabbled and argued all the time. That's how they related. I was always afraid of their fights. If there was a fight, I'd walk away. I never wanted to marry if marriage meant fighting. I just kept hoping that things would get better with Sally if I just gave her enough time and space."

Sally took the toddler and went camping for two months across the United States, leaving the teenagers in Michael's care. When she telephoned, Michael would listen to her description of the stars and tell her to have a good time. Nonetheless, as a single parent balancing family and career, Michael was very troubled.

When she returned from camping at the end of the summer, Sally and Michael were invited by a neighbor, the divorced father of one of their son's friends, to join him and his children for a week of sailing at his summer home on Nantucket. He also owned a chalet in Vail, Colorado, and maintained a yacht and villa in the Virgin Islands.

Behind in his office work due to his household responsibilities, Michael encouraged Sally and their son Charlie to go without him. Again, Sally telephoned him with glowing descriptions of a wonderful time, and extended the vacation. But when she returned home, Sally told Michael that she wanted a divorce. In fact, she moved in with her new lover just two blocks away, a situation that caused Charlie profound anguish.

Michael immediately saw a psychologist for counseling, who told him, after meeting with Sally, that the marriage could not be saved. Devastated, Michael started a cycle of physical decline. Never overweight, he lost 30 pounds and developed a jaundiced complexion and chronic insomnia. Physicians had no answer for him. As he recalled these hard times, Michael's face grew red and he began to cry.

He swiveled around in his desk chair and gained some control of his emotions. "I loved her," Michael said simply. "I still love what she once was. I could have accepted her death because death is a part of life. When you're in love and married, you fear and dread death for yourself and your spouse. But you know it's inevitable. I hurt every minute and wanted it all to be just a nightmare. I was exhausted because I could never sleep. Yet I could never get out of bed in the morning. I would sit and stare out the window. I did nothing. My sister and brother would stop by every morning just to get me on my feet."

Plagued with these symptoms over many months, Michael changed therapists. He began seeing a female psychologist who made him feel comfortable about expressing his emotions. "She would ask me what I had accomplished that day. When I'd say that I got out of bed, dressed, and drove to see her, she would say that was wonderful. The male therapist I had never seemed accepting of me. Even though he didn't say anything, I felt judged, that I had to measure up."

But Michael credited his 15-year-old son Charlie with bringing him to his senses. "One night I was in such a shambles that I wanted to kill that guy [his wife's lover]. I wanted to knock on his door and hit him with a tire jack. I was out of control. My son was terrorized and started to cry. He stayed with me and held me. I suddenly realized that I had to stay well and alive for my children. I had reached bottom. I couldn't allow myself to disintegrate anymore."

After that incident, Michael started to move forward slowly with his therapist. He began to accept responsibility for making choices about his future. However, as in Stephen Marshall's case, he did not believe in a total cure. Eight years after his divorce, Michael occasionally sees Sally and her husband at high school swimming matches rooting for Michael and Sally's daughter. "I still can't stand to see that guy with his arm around Sally. But I'm able to focus better now and not let things like that debilitate me. I am finally learning to think about myself and am having some happy years."

"Go Live in a Hovel"

Ex-husbands whom I talked with worried about living in a permanent state of despair when they first realized that their wives were cheating on them. They felt helpless about initiating any action, and often escaped into lonely silence. They could not imagine ever plunging into life again, even for the sake of maintaining old ties or forming new friendships.

Three months after his separation, for example, Jerry Fusione did not want to talk to anyone. He credited loyal employees with maintaining his business. "I was all right for only about three hours a day." After his wife Peggy told him on the tennis court that she wanted a divorce, Jerry was unable to leave the house, only venturing outside to see a lawyer. He and Peggy also met with a psychologist, who told Jerry that the marriage was irreconcilable.

"I have experienced the death of loved ones," Jerry explained, "but divorce was the most traumatic experience I have ever had. I felt dead myself." The first Christmas on his own, Jerry drove from his home in Ohio to stay by himself in a simple cabin in Lewistown, Maine. "I didn't want any part of Christmas Day. But the second year was better because I had the kids." The time in between Christmases, Jerry sat on a stool at the end of any bar, talking to no one. "The hardest thing I had to deal with," Jerry continued, "was my own apathy. I couldn't spin away from it."

At first, Jerry depended solely on the advice of his attorney. It was hard for him to admit a need for psychological counseling. Accustomed to being in control of his life, he had difficulty accepting and expressing how he felt. Furthermore, he had to understand and cope with deep personal guilt from earlier years.

Jerry and Peggy: The Beginning

Within two years of their marriage in 1972, Jerry and Peggy, college sweethearts with graduate degrees, had it all together for their age—they had a baby, a new furnished house, and two cars. But at age 30, Jerry had an affair. The "Rabbit Angstrom" of his generation, Jerry, an ex-basketball and baseball star, lost athletic pride. "Turning 30 was a big shock for me. My body wouldn't respond as it once had, and I needed attention. I figured that I was fourth on Peggy's list behind the kids, family, and house. I found a woman who offered me the attention I craved. When Peggy found out what I was doing, I stopped seeing this woman. Peggy and I were in counseling for months and pulled things back together, or so I thought."

For the next three years, Jerry felt that he and Peggy had strong communication. But on a December afternoon in 1982, Jerry arrived home unannounced to find Peggy in bed with a neighbor, "a guy who has a reputation for being a womanizer. Obviously, I was upset, but I thought it was just a sexual thing and let it pass without too much trouble."

Jerry did not think to ask Peggy why she wanted to be caught. The incident made him aware, nevertheless, that Peggy had not recovered from his affair as easily as he had assumed. But Jerry was distracted from pursuing these insights in more depth due to his efforts to expand his business when interest rates were at 22 percent. Absorbed in his financial problems, Jerry was less attentive to family conversations at dinner. He did not hear about parents' night at school, and felt cheated that he did not attend. Still, Jerry never thought that his marriage was on the rocks until the actual separation.

Playing tennis one spring morning, Peggy stormed off the court. "I want a divorce!" she exclaimed. "I can't live with you." Beyond this outburst, Jerry claims that she did not tell him why. But she did say that she was going with a friend, an antiques dealer, on a weekend buying trip to Chicago. Jerry did not object, for he was glad to put some distance between them, thinking it would ease the tension somewhat. When Peggy returned, Jerry asked about a strange key on her dresser. She answered that he really would not want to know about it. But rifling through her address book, Jerry deduced that it opened the apartment door of a friend of his, a divorced man living on Lakeshore Drive. Needless to say, the antiques dealer knew nothing about the Chicago trip. Given that knowledge, Jerry sought out a lawyer.

* * *

In hindsight, Jerry realized that his marriage ended in 1976 with his own affair, for Peggy never regained faith and trust in him. Her insecurity was also rekindled by their risky financial state. Besides dealing with the loss of his children and home, Jerry had to come to terms with the knowledge that his own infidelity was the initial cause of his unraveling marriage.

"My father died when I was 17, and my son essentially lost contact with me at age 12," he reflected. "I felt real guilt for any of my actions that contributed to this. This was the worst period of my life. I kept worrying, 'Am I a bad person? Is this all my fault?' I had no ego. The only thing that challenged me to get better were Peggy's final words to me—'Go live in a hovel!'"

For a while, the divorce process was therapeutic for Jerry because it forced him to focus. He treated divorce like a business deal. For example, he enjoyed working with his attorney to decide how the children could best be protected. He had no problem agreeing that Peggy should stay with them in the family home. He rented a small apartment in the same neighborhood in order to be nearby. "But I was impatient to get the kids back. Peggy told them I wouldn't care about them once I left. My lawyer told me to be patient, but that was very hard. I wanted to pick up the phone and scream at her."

The divorce process helped Jerry to think clearly about his family responsibilities, but didn't give him mechanisms to cope with his anger, grief, and guilt. He avoided psychological counseling for months until he was finally forced to admit that he was growing more and more isolated. Therapy helped him treat divorce like a personal crisis, not just a business deal. In discussions with his therapist, he worked on ways to handle his resentment toward Peggy. He knew he had to practice new ways of communicating with her if he wanted to remain involved with the daily lives of his children. "Even now, we can't really be friends," Jerry remarked, "but we have learned to cooperate for the sake of the kids."

Jerry appreciated therapy for helping him confront the demons in his past, which he was ignoring in favor of blaming Peggy for their breakup. He admitted that when he was 30, he should have talked with Peggy about how changes in his athletic ability troubled him. He knew that his affair was a way of proving his sexual stamina. He acknowledged that had he been more open about expressing these fears, Peggy might have confided her own. But in his conversations with me, he tried not to dwell on how past problems could have been averted.

As a result of therapy, Jerry learned to accept his role as a divorced single parent. He developed new friendships among divorced men and women who shared his concerns. Feeling their approval, he began to feel better about himself. Single for five years, Jerry recently married a woman "who believes in herself and her capabilities. A woman has to have her own self-worth and not depend solely on her husband or other men to provide it." Jerry has few misgivings about his future.

Pas de Corps to Pas de Deux

In all divorces, mutual fault exists. When husbands and wives verbalize their tension, honesty often draws them together, even while they are discussing what separates them most. Yet, sidestepping such genuine moments is a particular skill of troubled couples.

For example, silence reigned at the Fusiones' dinner table most nights. From the moment that Peggy stalked from the tennis court demanding a divorce, the conversation never continued. When Jerry asked about the mysterious key, she answered that he really would not want to know about it. Husbands, as well as wives, can manipulate events not only through silence, but by allowing things to happen, letting them go, and wearing bandages across their eyes.

Author Edith Wharton described this syndrome in *A Custom of the Country*, a novel published in 1913. One of her characters, Ralph Merel, would not confront his wife with his suspicions of her adultery because

> . . . he dared not face the truth. But he knew this was not
> the case. It was not the truth he feared, it was another
> lie . . . She would go on eluding and doubting, watching
> him as he watched her. . . .

Wharton's insight into masculine behavior is a starting point for understanding 55-year-old Phil Garrison, the president of a small manufacturing company, who still describes his ex-wife June as the "perfect wife and mother." It was a long time before he figured out that the relationship between June and his newfound best friend was not as innocent as he had thought. But he wondered if the real turning point in his marriage did not occur 18 years earlier, after the birth of their fourth child.

When they were married, Phil aspired to an upper-middle-class income, an attractive home, two children, and a dog. He achieved all of these goals. But when June, who wanted six children, became pregnant for the fourth time, Phil insisted that she have an abortion. "I couldn't maintain our lifestyle and afford to send any more kids to college. We had a lot of arguments." Phil reached for a cigarette. "But I finally accepted the fact that she would have the child."

After the baby's birth, Phil had a vasectomy without telling June. His secret was exposed only because he developed an infection. He now marks this incident as the beginning of the end of their marriage. June lost trust in him for not involving her in his decision. Furthermore, she was profoundly disappointed by not being able to have more children.

However, Phil never considered his marriage to be in real trouble until ten years later when their minister introduced them to the Scotts, a wealthy young couple, new to town, who had joined their church. The Garrisons and Scotts were soon seeing each other not only on Sunday mornings but four nights a week.

Henry Scott, an advertising executive, was flashy with his money, picking up dinner checks and using his expense account to entertain the Garrisons for three-day weekends at fancy resorts. Phil thought the two couples got along great together. Then over drinks one evening, the bandages fell from his eyes. He noticed that within the quartet, June and Henry were having a private time exchanging secret glances and furtive smiles. But Phil never uttered a word to June about his uneasiness. He even accepted another invitation to be guests of the Scotts for a week at their condominium in Boca Raton, Florida. Sitting on their balcony, he had a clear view of Henry and June talking nonstop in the middle of the pool. Their relaxed intimacy made him uncomfortable, but Phil never uttered a word to June. Protecting herself in the shade, Henry's wife remained immersed in the fictional world of Danielle Steel.

A few days later, Phil suffered a heart attack and had bypass surgery. His convalescence severed the quartet, but not the relationship between Henry and June. Phil endured watching June, outside of his hearing, have endless telephone conversations with Henry. But Phil never commented.

To celebrate Phil's recovery, Henry invited the Garrisons to join him and Sandy at a four-day convention for advertising executives in Scottsdale, Arizona. In the bar one evening after dinner, Phil said he was tired and wanted to turn in. June responded that she and Henry would stay and dance. But Phil was stern and steered her firmly to the elevator. In their bedroom, June offered yet another scenario. She intended to accompany Henry to his morning meetings. Phil finally blew up.

"What the hell's going on? You are not going with him. Why doesn't his own wife go?"

June's answer was simple. "She doesn't want to."

Waking up during the night, Phil realized that June was gone. Not the innocent Juliet, she was leaning over the balcony, talking in mid-air to Henry, who also balanced precariously. "Get your ass back in bed,"

Phil roared. June quickly complied, but the confrontation had no second act.

Phil wearily explained, "I could never believe that my good Christian wife, whom I loved, could ever be unfaithful to me. I thought she was infatuated, and I didn't want to push anymore."

A direct clash did occur a few weeks later when Phil and June had dinner reservations to celebrate the purchase of her new car. Phil remembered that she looked particularly beautiful. While he was dressing, June said she needed to make a quick trip to the supermarket. In the manner of a private detective in a cheap novel, Phil followed her in his car, finally spotting June's new Honda parked next to Henry's Cadillac Seville. Growing red and tearful at the memory, Phil cleared his throat. "I couldn't believe what I was seeing."

He watched Henry and June drive in their respective cars to the darkest part of the shopping center, where they sat together in Henry's front seat. With great difficulty, Phil continued his story. "I was breathing so hard. I couldn't believe this was happening to me. I went home because I thought they would have to head there. But June didn't return for two more hours, too late for us to still go out for dinner."

June apologized, saying that she had met Henry at the supermarket and was detained because he had wanted to test-drive the car on the open highway. Phil claimed that the speedometer never registered such mileage. "I grabbed her by the throat, said, 'You're a fucking liar,' pulled down her pants and put my hand between her legs. If she had had sex, she had cleared up the evidence." June promised that she would never see Henry again, the man she once had called Phil's best friend.

But telephone bills indicated that their relationship was still on. When Phil and June went West on an extended vacation, June used the telephone charge card to call Henry's office. Suspicious of her frequent disappearances into telephone booths, Phil asked to see the monthly statements, as June managed the household accounts. Phil also learned that before attending church on Sundays, June and Henry would have coffee at the local hospital, where June volunteered. Then they would join the other half of the quartet at services. Phil could bear the duplicity no longer. He saw an attorney to file for divorce. Hysterical, June swore that her relationship with Henry would end. Eager to give his marriage another chance, Phil asked the attorney to send a bill for the hours he had spent with him.

But two months later, June moved into the guest bedroom because Phil's snoring bothered her. Phil commented ironically, "Funny that it hadn't bothered her for the first 25 years." Suspecting that Henry and June had been together while he was on business trips, Phil hid voice-activated tape recorders throughout the house. He caught Henry's voice in the garage, saying, "I have to get the fuck out of here."

"This," Phil rolled his eyes, "from the Christian gentleman I never once heard swear." Phil had never believed that Henry and June were having sex until the tape picked up a reference that she made to a magazine article on female orgasm. Her magic words were, "But Henry, every time we have sex, I have an orgasm." Finally convinced, Phil went back to see his lawyer and moved out of the house.

Eight months later during his conversations with me, Phil was taking Valium and had lost 30 pounds. He was not in therapy because the "therapists I saw in the past never said a thing." But he does recall one psychologist telling him, "Your wife is using you as a meal ticket. You mean little else to her." Another therapist, a woman whom he described as a "Ph.D. with fat legs," listened, and merely remarked, "If you think your wife is not having an affair, you're crazy."

Phil did not believe that therapy or a relationship with another woman would help him. "I just don't know how to get myself better," he worried. "I can think of other things now, but these problems are on my mind 100 times a day. My manhood has been destroyed. I've been with a lot of beautiful, wealthy women who are anxious for a monogamous relationship. They are willing to crawl into bed. It doesn't mean anything to me, but it's given me my ego back a little bit, helps my self-esteem. That's therapy for me." In terms of recovery, Phil figured that he was at square one and a half. "What can I say? I still love the woman."

If he was going to achieve any peace, Phil had to deal with the complexity of the person June had become. He had never pursued the idea that June's affair might have been her way of solving her own problems, rather than a plot to destroy his masculinity for past mistakes. To accept himself as a "real man," he preferred his fantasy of

June as a "good Christian wife and mother." In fact, the very first time he saw June, the way she looked fulfilled some inarticulated dream.

* * *

At age 24, most of Phil's buddies were married. One Friday afternoon, walking into a favorite Philadelphia watering hole with a friend, he noticed an attractive young woman at the cigarette machine. "If you get me a girl like that one, then I'll consider getting married," Phil challenged. The terms made, Phil was introduced to June, and he took her home. They married two years later. During our conversation, Phil consistently referred to June as the "perfect bride and wife with absolutely no bad habits; she never smoked or drank. She was a perfect mother and housekeeper." June still lives with Henry, while Phil remains nostalgic for a simpler life.

At the time of our conversation, Phil had yet to distinguish between his imaginative conception of June and the real thing. Living with memories of his wife's innocence was a real death wish, for he was blinded from seeing opportunities for a new life.

Believing in the value of a wife's sexual fidelity, men of Phil's generation tend to define the success of their marriage on the basis of "Did she or didn't she?" If semen stains are missing, then the marriage must be intact. When Phil and June married in 1950, virginity was so exalted in a bride that for her not to remain a chaste wife would be the ultimate corruption of herself, the demise of the marriage, and the final disillusionment of the husband who was no longer able to cherish his image of the "perfect girl."

Men who have married in the past 20 years are no less disturbed by their wives' sexual liaisons. But they do not measure the decline and fall of their marriage solely on the basis of sexual fidelity. Nevertheless, research released in 1993 by The General Social Survey of the National Opinion Research Center of the University of Chicago suggests that extramarital affairs are more common among young people than those born before 1940. Fewer people age 50 or older report having had an affair.

Stephen Marshall, the young attorney whose wife left him for a TV anchor chair and an electronic guitarist, felt most betrayed, for example, because he and Ashley had made a pact before their wedding that they would not go to bed with another person or have an affair without admitting to each other the problems that made them want to do so. Cheating would not be their way of avoiding their marital tensions.

"An affair is symptomatic of something else that's wrong in a marriage," Stephen believed. "If that temptation ever existed, Ashley and I agreed not to betray and embarrass each other that way. We would confront the problems head-on, and if we couldn't work them out, then we would go our separate ways."

Younger men such as Stephen Marshall interpreted infidelity as a red flag signaling that a married couple must face some painful questions. An affair in itself does not have to be the end of a marriage if a couple is willing to admit and tackle the reasons that caused it. This conviction shared by younger men does not mean that they minimize the ethical importance of sexual commitment. But to value it as the sole defining quality of a good marriage can, ironically, stifle the communication that might eliminate the need for having the affair. Men younger than the generation of Phil Garrison believe in the ideal that husbands and wives ought to try to explain to each other the real reasons behind their sexual infidelity if they hope to reconcile with a new basis of trust.

Carving Out a Reconciliation

Another careful distinction is drawn between sexual infidelity and emotional betrayal by Gordon Tyndall, 44, nine years older than 35-year-old Stephen Marshall, and eleven years younger than 55-year-old Phil Garrison. When his wife Cindy told him that she wanted a divorce, Gordon claimed that it was no less shocking to hear her say that she did not love him than if he had walked into a bedroom and found her with a lover. He felt betrayed that Cindy responded to his failure to meet her needs by circumventing him and trusting another man. "I didn't care if she was sexually involved as much as I did that she could confide her deepest feelings in a man besides myself, and not give me any indication that I was disappointing her." An affair would not have rocked his marriage as much as Cindy's choosing to solve their marital problems in her own way.

For Gordon, Cindy's infidelity consisted of deceiving him that all was well between them. This rejection was the major reason why Gordon felt such deep bereavement when he moved from their home. The worst part was the "uncertainty that I would ever be whole again. I had developed a sense of myself up to the point of separation that had included a partner. Cindy and the kids were central to my life, my identity. It felt terrible to separate from a partner who I always thought I would share my existence with. My big concern was that I would never again fill that void."

But after a three-year separation, Gordon and Cindy grew in self-knowledge to the degree that they were able to confront and understand each other. Now they live together again as a family with their young son and daughter. Their reconciliation came about through tough introspection, not romantic escapism.

"It is not a magical reconciliation," Gordon offered, "but we have a better understanding of what happened three years ago and how to avoid reaching a point where we can't deal with each other. We're more openly expressive and tolerant."

* * *

The Tyndalls felt the first signs of tension during graduate school. Married immediately after college, Gordon worked as a technical writer, and Cindy taught elementary school. Then after two years, they left their jobs, enrolled in graduate programs, and lived on a limited budget. Their schedules conflicted because Cindy had day and evening courses in library science, while Gordon's time was consumed with research projects for a Ph.D. in public policy. They spent few weekends together.

During this time, Gordon had an affair with a fellow student, but denied it when Cindy became suspicious. Soon after, he had another relationship. Admitting their estrangement, Cindy and Gordon saw a marriage counselor who concluded that they were not happy together and should separate. But financially, they could not afford to live apart until completing their degrees. Instead, they agreed to live separate lives under the same roof, a terrible strain for both of them. Nevertheless, even with degrees in hand, they stayed together as a couple.

Gordon found it hard to explain why. "We weren't entirely happy with each other, but somehow we were comfortable. We were afraid of the unknown, of separation." Gordon even stopped seeing other women, for reasons that seemed perfectly rational to *him*: "In school, I didn't feel as if I were cheating, but not being a student, out in the real world, I felt guilty."

As they drifted back together, Cindy talked about having children. Once she was pregnant, Gordon was delighted about the prospect of being a father, and he remained faithful. They had another baby two years later. Gordon was, therefore, caught unawares when Cindy expressed profound unhappiness and expressed the desire to separate. "We were never model communicators," Gordon offered, "but I was flabbergasted. I had taken Cindy for granted. I thought we were moving in the same direction, on the same track. But she wasn't getting what she needed from me. She had only negative feedback, and wanted out."

They agreed to see a marriage counselor, who advised them to pay an attorney instead of him. This advice disappointed Gordon, who thought that he and Cindy were at the point of "opening up." But Cindy was adamant that "we are not getting anywhere." Their decision to separate was made in November, but Gordon did not move from the house until after the Christmas holidays so that they could celebrate as a family.

Gordon did not go into therapy, but counseling services for Families in Transition helped him to support the children emotionally and, indirectly, himself. For the first few months, he felt as if he were "in a maelstrom. The one strong focus that I was able to maintain was that the kids would not be harmed by this. Everything else was confusing, and I didn't know what I was doing. I was tired and numb, mostly numb, for eight months."

He gained emotional control as he developed new insights into what had actually happened between him and Cindy. "I spent time looking into myself. I gained a better handle on both the positive and negative things in our marriage." To accomplish this task, Gordon read books on divorce, and also some on the mourning process that a person experiences when a spouse dies. Lillian B. Rubin's book, *Intimate Strangers: Men & Women Together,* was especially helpful to him due to the inclusion of the case studies on men.

Simultaneously, Cindy was gaining a new understanding of their marriage through psychoanalysis. From their fresh perspectives, Cindy and Gordon were willing to talk to each other again in an effort to rebuild their marriage. Gordon admitted to Cindy that he had done a great deal to injure her. He began to correct nonverbal cues in his behavior and express his feelings more openly.

Gordon concluded, for example, that after the birth of their children, life was comfortable for him in a new home with a family. But Cindy did not sense that she had his love or respect. Gordon's way of making her feel special was to give her gifts that he had made. "I liked to make things out of wood for Cindy and the kids." He looked at his hands. "I thought I was giving her things of value, because I treasure things that my father had carved for me. But this was not the case with Cindy." For her birthday, Gordon gave Cindy (an expert chef), a knife rack he had designed and carved. Cindy's appreciation seemed to be sincere. However, in a counseling session with Gordon much later, she revealed that she considered his carving of the knife rack to have been a convenient outlet for his own self-expression, not a testimony of his love for her. Gordon offered the incident as an example of their inability to tell each other what they valued and felt.

Through psychoanalysis, Cindy came to realize that she had self-esteem issues stemming from her perception that her parents were too critical of her as a child. Sublimating her anger toward them for many years, Cindy projected these feelings onto Gordon. Furthermore, Gordon contributed to her low self-image as a result of his relationships with other women during graduate school. Not wanting to dominate, manipulate, or indulge in self-flagellation, Gordon and Cindy are starting over again with a new understanding of themselves and each other.

* * *

Gordon did not feel that he was subverting his manliness by returning to Cindy and confessing equal culpability in their near breakup. But his attitude is rare. By the time most husbands gain insight into why their marriages did not work, opportunities for reconciliation have passed by. Ex-husbands whose wives have left them for another man have said to me, "I still love the woman." They even hope that someday they will be a couple again, without having to invest any effort in understanding what caused their marriage to fall apart. Years have passed without their moving beyond name-calling and blame.

But, in the imaginations of these spurned husbands, an ex-wife must first be punished before he will accept her back. They recover their manhood by fantasizing that she is in a helpless position, deserted by her lover, and walking the streets without even the skills of a bag lady. Rescued from the church shelter by her former husband's offer of remarriage, the chagrined and chastened wife gratefully returns.

"Was That You?"

Few ex-husbands are willing to become doormats to woo their wives away from lovers, but they can be incredibly resilient in their attempts to avoid divorce. Colin Perkins, age 48, tolerated his wife's infidelity for over 20 years before ending their marriage. With a twinkle in his eye, Colin enjoyed seeing the effect that his words had on me: "My wife had only one bad habit. She kept falling in love with her tennis partners, but she didn't play mixed doubles."

Colin and Alice had eloped during their senior year in college because she was pregnant, but it was not a shotgun wedding. Their earlier efforts to marry had been halted by Alice's father on the basis of their youth. Colin's first troubling insight into Alice's attraction to younger women occurred in a supermarket when they were newlyweds. Colin knew that Alice was "really getting excited about the girl captain of the local high school tennis team." She was a star in their New Jersey bedroom community whose daytime population was composed of young matrons who enjoyed tennis and swimming.

As they were picking over the veggies, Alice innocently blurted, "That's Molly Brannigan over there. She's really exciting to play tennis with."

"It was as if a movie star had walked in," Colin remembered. "That night we talked about her feelings, but I don't think that Alice knew at that time that she had lesbian tendencies. I wasn't sure myself. I didn't want to dwell on it. I put the incident in the back of my mind."

However, by their tenth anniversary, Colin was aware of five tennis players who were special in Alice's life. Letters passed twice a day, for example, between her and a young woman who was traveling the world in tournaments. Colin recalled denying to himself the possibility of his wife's having sexual relations with these women. "I tried to pass them off as crushes or intense friendships."

The relationship that most damaged Colin's ego occurred when Alice offered hollow excuses for not moving with him from New Jersey to Chicago when he was given a corporate promotion. Her rationalizations could not hide the fact that she was reluctant to leave a lover. In the three months that they lived apart, Colin found reassuring comfort with another woman, his first affair. When Alice finally arrived in Chicago, he told her that he had long been aware of her sexual relations with women.

During this period of their lives, Colin spent $50,000 on therapy for Alice, and at least $10,000 on himself. "I kept thinking that something must be wrong with me. I'm obviously doing something wrong. And once you start thinking like that, you can come up a thousand things that you need to explore. I think that both of us spent a lot of time, energy, and money trying to make things work. You have to understand that I really cared about Alice's welfare, and I wanted things to be right for her and for us."

It took ten more years for Colin to admit, "I was her camouflage." But Colin continued to offer generous hospitality in their home for women tennis players visiting Chicago for tournaments. When Alice told him that she was going to attend a weekend tennis camp with Charlotte, one of the players, Colin blanched. Alice assured him, "This is like your fishing buddies, or going to a hockey game with your brother."

Not comforted by these analogies, Colin snooped through Alice's closet that Saturday morning. He discovered a shoe box brimming with love letters from the woman Alice was away with, plus Alice's diary filled with details of explicit sex. Devastated, Colin not only felt that he had failed in his marriage but that he did not know how to help Alice. "I was angry, jealous, and hurt. The worst part was that I didn't know what to do." Nevertheless, Colin maintained an outrageous sense of humor to pull off a practical joke that allowed him a measure of satisfaction.

He figured that Alice and Charlotte would not return until late Sunday night because "they would want to spend the last possible minute with each other." He unplugged the electric eye on the garage and closed the bolt locks on all of the outside doors. Fumbling in the middle of the night, Alice finally had to ring the doorbell. Colin took pleasure in facing Charlotte to ask in mock innocence, "Did you have a good time?" Although he felt terrible, he had to figure some way to lighten up the situation.

By Monday afternoon, Colin had seen an attorney and was back with his psychiatrist. Alice moved out to live with Charlotte, but was home within months, promising that their relationship was over. Colin thought otherwise. On a fishing trip one weekend with his son, Colin resorted to another practical joke. If Charlotte was on the scene again, he knew that she and Alice would snuggle in the living room, listening to Linda Ronstadt tapes. In the middle of one tape, Colin spliced a few seconds of a woman climaxing from the "Sounds of Love" series. "I got such psychic mileage from that, instant gratification. I was tortured. I felt absolutely distraught, but I would laugh uproariously, thinking about Alice and Charlotte, startled, asking, 'Was that you?'" The tape was missing when Colin returned, confirming that Alice and Charlotte were an item again.

Without Charlotte, Alice was miserable. Life also seemed bleak for Colin, who still loved Alice. Consequently, he invited Charlotte to move in with Alice and him. "I didn't want to look back in five years," he reasoned, "and wonder if I really tried everything to make our marriage work. Alice just couldn't give up either of us."

It is a pale hypothesis to suggest that Colin was so deeply hurt by Alice's preference of a woman over himself, that by agreeing to this living arrangement he was hoping that Alice would see the light and choose him. But in a way, Colin achieved his goal, as Charlotte did move out, unable to share Alice with Colin.

Colin hoped that he and Alice were off to a brand new start. They spent a romantic four days at a Tucson resort, but driving home from the airport, Alice began to cry upon hearing the voice of Linda Ronstadt on the radio. Colin tried again. "Okay. I'll offer you one more deal. If it doesn't work, we'll dissolve the marriage as smoothly and cleanly as possible." He asked Alice not to make any attempt to communicate with Charlotte. He promised to help her through a mourning period by being a sympathetic, nonjudgmental listener. Alice agreed, but did respond, "I just don't know that I can feel the sexual things about a man that I did with Charlotte."

Two months later, Colin arrived home from a European business trip a day earlier than expected and found Charlotte and Alice "scared in bed together." Colin described himself as suddenly feeling a great sense of calm. "I hung up my garment bag, turned around, and said, 'Don't worry about it.' I knew I would see an attorney in the morning. I had done everything that I possibly could do. I had exhausted the possibilities."

On the airplane returning home, Colin had torn an advertisement for Nike shoes out of a magazine. A young man with a determined posture was walking away from a deserted locker room toward a doorway filled with light. The caption read: "Just do it, but do it right."

Colin handed me the ripped magazine page that he kept in his office desk as a talisman. The message helped him through the worst days of his separation. "I couldn't even enjoy doing the things I always liked doing by myself. Watching my son trout fishing in the Rockies, I'd find myself thinking, Wait until I tell Alice about this. It took about a year before I could do everyday things without thinking about her and wanting to share them. Now I have some peace. I still love her, and I don't want anything to happen to her."

Colin used considerable detail to draw us into the scenario of his marriage. But he did not want to exploit melodrama and pity. Neither did he offer penetrating insights into why he tolerated living with such an arrangement. But he was eager to talk with me in order to offer other men hope that they can overcome seemingly hopeless marital situations without either self-destructing or destroying the dignity of their wives.

* * *

The first impulse of many men who are rejected by their wives is to cut themselves off from the world, to carry their grief in silence. They isolate themselves from love altogether, and stumble on, alone.

Guilt resulting from past behavior is often a powerful counterforce against their self-acceptance. But the saddest thing about men who reluctantly divorce is a tendency to become more estranged and helpless as time goes on. Their response is often to disguise reality by being either sentimental or cynical about what they cannot change. Only when they see through their defenses and open up to new possibilities do they discover their capacity for renewal.

For some divorced men, this never happens. Years after the divorce, they still keep fighting and remain fixated on their former wife's transgressions. But men who do recover from the anguish of a wife's betrayal invest time and energy into the process of getting well. They do this in a variety of constructive ways that will be discussed in Part 2 of *Men on Divorce*. Having undergone a great deal of pain, they come to terms with infidelity and learn of "finalities besides the grave." Men trust in love as women do and assume the risk that it will always be returned. And when it is not, human heartache is the same.

LONG-SUFFERING HUSBANDS

It is only kind of you, Libby, to feel that I would
want to know that I am off the hook. But I'm not,
I can't be, I don't even want to be—not until I
make some sense of the larger hook I'm on.
                                    Yours,
                                        Gabe

from *Letting Go*, by Philip Roth

IN LEGEND AND REAL LIFE, the long-suffering woman who endures her husband's alcoholism, carousing, brutality, or indifference out of fear, obedience, economic dependency, or love has long been in our consciousness. For the past 30 years, sympathetic efforts to expose the oppression of women have focused on wives as the victims and survivors of divorce. That a husband might also feel alienated, helpless, invisible, or abused is somehow beyond popular belief.

Stereotypes of male/female behavior are threatened, for example, when one of the nation's leading jurists refers to himself as having been an "abused man" from the day of his wedding 35 years ago.

* * *

Ambrose Wilkie talked to his parents a week before his wedding ceremony about backing out. But his father, fearing embarrassment, convinced him otherwise. Ambrose had a mercurial romance with Joan Patton all through college. But even though they were never a passionate couple, marriage was inevitable during their senior year. Both virgins, Ambrose described their honeymoon as "disastrous. We could never have a good time together, and that started very early."

Ambrose recalled a simple surprise birthday party he arranged for

Joan when they were newlyweds. Friends greeted her with wine and cheese when she arrived home from work. But instead of appreciating Ambrose for his thoughtfulness, she berated him. He remembered, "She was so pissed off because she had to clean up the apartment afterwards. She thought it was an awful thing for me to have done. Even the last time I talked with her, two years ago, she brought up that party again. I could never give Joan anything, not even a present. And she never did anything nice for me; she never gave me anything or surprised me. If I gave her anything, she'd just get pissed off."

Christmas gifts were very prosaic. If Ambrose gave Joan clothes, she returned them to the store. For five straight years, she gave him itchy wool shirts that he could never wear. Exasperated, he recalled a cameo he had bought for her in Pompeii but that she left behind in a Rome hotel and never tried to recover.

Ambrose and Joan had five adult children, "but it was Russian roulette. We couldn't really make love. Maybe once a month. If she did have a good time during sex, then she would be vicious for weeks. She just beat the hell out of me, not physically, but I was always clobbered. She never showed affection—no hugging or kissing—not even with the children. I lost my balls over this thing. She said if she cleaned the house, that was love, and she didn't have to tell me."

Ambrose could not be himself with Joan. Their conversations were as unspontaneous as their sex life. Ambrose could never share his secrets or worries because "she would just zap me, cut me off with a curt or demeaning remark that I was a weakling and couldn't cope with much." Had Joan not become pregnant during their first year, Ambrose wondered if they might well have separated. "Then again," he reflected, "I didn't believe in divorce. But more important, I kept living in anticipation. I thought things would get better. My anticipation exceeded reality. I kept working for tomorrow, hoping that Joan would be nice and gentle."

But Joan never offered gentleness, not even when Ambrose was mugged late one night in the courthouse parking lot. Hospitalized for a week with a concussion, unable to speak and unaware of his name, Ambrose elicited little sympathy from Joan, except for her unemotional admonishment, "You'll be all right."

Ambrose identified Joan's indifference to his injuries as the turning point in his efforts to maintain their marriage. Most evenings, he returned to his office, checking the work that law clerks had churned out, preparing for the next day in court, and writing essays for scholarly legal journals. Conversation at home was limited, and family meals were a rare occurrence, as was sex.

Ambrose's recognition as an authority on a specialized point in international law earned him a worldwide reputation. In 1985, he gave the keynote address for an international seminar in London. Ambrose maintained that after this success, "Joan never smiled at me again. She was rude to my colleagues, made fun of their wives, and essentially demeaned me. But her final words of wisdom were: 'The world thinks so highly of you, Charlie, but my role is to keep things in perspective for you.' I was never an egomaniac about my success," Ambrose explained. "Yet it did become my only source of self-confidence. I continued to get along with Joan only by evasion."

Ambrose spoke before international audiences, but his world at home grew smaller and smaller. Social invitations dwindled because the Wilkies never reciprocated. "It was always too much trouble for Joan to entertain at home. We never even had our families. I like the arts, but she developed a supercilious attitude toward them, even though she was enrolled in a graduate English program. In fact, the only people who ever visited our home were Joan's graduate student friends. I didn't want to go to the theater or museums by myself. Except for my work, I was absolutely shut off from life. I had no confidence in myself, except for what I achieved professionally. Even worse, Joan and I had nothing to talk about. The children fended for themselves. Oh, once in a while she'd cook a bloody chicken."

Sex occurred so rarely that Ambrose and Joan finally consulted a sex therapist. "Well, when we got through A, B, C, and D, we were to go home and practice. It was ridiculous. I couldn't make love to someone that I had grown not to like," Ambrose muttered.

Yet they stayed married. Ambrose began seeing other women, "fine ladies who helped me to have a better sense of myself. I began to realize that sex was a wonderful thing, and I was pretty good at it. I abdicated at home. But really I was only acting the way that I had been treated for 30 years."

Joan moved out of their home one spring evening when Ambrose made mention of the "crush" she seemed to have on an omnipresent graduate student, 15 years her junior. By that time, any issue would have pulled the trigger. But after their separation, Ambrose felt very lonely. "I thought I had lost it and would always be solitary and on the fringe of things."

He attributed his spiritual rejuvenation to psychotherapy and his reading of the works and life of Thomas Merton, "a thoughtful philosopher, a quirky guy who should never have been a monk. I enjoyed reading about him. I stopped reading junk. For example, I gained a great deal of insight from Carl Lewin's *The Heritage of Illusions*. I found my way to the arts and started back to church. Years earlier, Joan had come out of the closet as an atheist, and had made fun of religion."

Through psychoanalysis, Ambrose learned that his depression was situational, tied to his unhappy marriage. He relished the insights he gained, and learned to see himself more clearly: "It was a beautiful moment when the psychiatrist told me that I was as sound as a dollar except for dealing with my wife." But Ambrose truly appreciated that he was recovering from self-doubt when early one morning, two years after his separation, he realized that he had spent the previous evening reading at home rather than returning to his office to bury himself in his work.

If he could relive his life, Ambrose says he would never have married Joan. He wishes that he had been more sure of himself at age 22 and not have allowed his father to persuade him differently. From the very beginning, his marriage fell far below his expectations, but "I kept believing in tomorrow. We had young kids and not much money until the last ten years. I kept thinking that things would get better with Joan. In time, I wasn't as committed. But for almost 30 years, I was loyal and took shit for it over and over again."

If he had left Joan in the early years, Ambrose claims that the agony would have been minimized for both of them. "Marriage that demands a lot of adjustments may be okay; but only if you have a lot of common ground and really like each other, can you really fly. If you don't enjoy today, tomorrow is going to be much worse."

Finishing our interview, Ambrose hurried from his office to catch an airplane for New York City with the new woman in his life, an advertising executive whom he will soon marry. He told me their plans for attending the theater, restaurants, and museums. "My first wife would not have enjoyed any of that. When we did go to museums, she would go off by herself. I always forgave her inability to show her love for me because I always thought she was doing the best she could. Then it became obvious to me that I was chasing a rainbow that didn't exist."

* * *

A life of resignation is often associated more with the experience of women in marriage who live in hope that "things will change" or choose not to test their options. Husbands are not perceived as needing a wife's reinforcement to validate their self-worth. But the reality is that brilliant, respected, and handsome men such as Ambrose Wilkie do lose self-esteem when underminded by a fault-finding wife. A successful career in itself was not enough to sustain his sense of personal goodness. No matter the praise they receive from the public, both men and women question their purpose and breed self-doubt when consistently criticized or mocked by a spouse.

The reasons that husbands and wives endure such marriages reveal the similarities, as opposed to the differences, in their complex psychological responses. Husbands also choose to avoid marital conflict by evasion and passive resistance, behavior traditionally assumed to be feminine. To live in expectation of love is a human condition, not a need assigned by gender.

The Role of the Caretaker

Similarly, some questions of conscience that husbands face in marriage are often more identified with the responsibilities of wives. In truth, the female function of caretaker and the male role of provider are only different versions of each other. For example, an altruistic spirit is traditionally valued as the defining quality of a good wife. This standard will often pose moral problems for a women who also wants to be independent and self-assertive. To balance caring for others with caring for oneself is accurately identified as the special problem of women. Yet, husbands are also familiar with the stress involved in deciding how much they should subordinate their own needs in order to support the needs of their wives.

Robert Fenner, age 50, spent lonely years trying to resolve this conflict. Even now he has no regrets about having married the woman that he did 26 years ago.

An only child, Robert was happy to meet Lois Leach, a college senior who came from a large family. Although eight years older than she, he felt no generational conflict between either Lois or her parents, except to observe that Mr. Leach was strict and Mrs. Leach, compliant.

Robert and Lois enthusiastically planned a candlelight wedding, but within a few years, the romance of their marriage started to flicker. Problems began when Lois suffered migraine headaches that required narcotic painkillers. The couple had wanted a large family but were advised by physicians that Lois should not have any more pregnancies, so they were content to have had two children.

Life with the Fenners soon became regimented around the cycle of Lois's headaches. Robert, the president of his family's prosperous furniture manufacturing company, would arrive home to eat casseroles sent in by neighbors, take care of the children, and wait for the doctor to stop by. "Daily living became predictable and strained, but I hardly had time to think about it," Robert said reflectively. "Lois's headaches were so bad that she would bang her head against the wall. A normal life was when she was out of bed, living on painkillers. We searched out the best medical advice. Surgery finally helped but didn't solve the problem."

Between 1975 and 1989, when they separated, Robert admitted sharing happy moments as well as terrible times with Lois. In an up-cycle, they would entertain at home, enjoy dinner out with friends, and motor-boat with their children on the waterways near their North Carolina home. Yet harmony was impossible to sustain because Lois was never well enough to participate in day-to-day decisions, and Robert kept undercutting himself by trying to involve her in them. For example, if he wanted to add a new sundeck to the house, Lois would never discuss the matter or state her preferences. "Conversations would end with, 'I don't feel well. Do what you want.'"

But Lois's lack of assertiveness troubled Robert even early in their marriage. "In many ways, the first year was the most difficult because I would become angry with Lois for lacking self-confidence. Yet we both realized that this was how she had been raised. Her mother was happy to say, 'Yes, dear,' to all of her husband's decisions. Lois's father raised his daughter to be the same way. For the first 10 to 15 years, I wanted Lois to be more assertive. But when doctors told me that her headaches could be stress induced, I backed away from insisting that Lois make decisions with me. Gradually, I took advantage of making all the decisions, and she didn't protest. I didn't think that a marriage should work this way, but I never admitted it. I wanted to keep the family intact."

Lois was more willing to accept professional counseling than Robert. Eventually, he also saw a psychologist, but without positive results. "I bared my soul because I knew things about me disturbed Lois. But finally I gave up because my therapist never responded to me, never offered any input. I wanted to understand what I did that provoked Lois's headaches."

Lois enrolled in an informal stress management course at a local hospital but disappointed Robert when she dropped out. After the children left for college, Robert agreed with Lois that a smaller home would be less of a burden to manage. They had moved into separate bedrooms a year earlier, so a new home promised little happiness. But even in new surroundings, Lois described her tension as too much to bear, and asked Robert to leave. They agreed to wait a few months in order to celebrate Thanksgiving and Christmas as a family. On January 3, 1990, Robert left.

Soberly, he confided, "It was hard for me to absorb that my very physical presence caused Lois stress. As soon as I was gone, she told me that she felt better. All the years that she was sick, my world shrank. Any social life we did have was as a family. Lois and I hadn't had an intimate relationship for years. I had such low self-esteem. I hadn't been in the singles' scene for 26 years. The first night I was in my apartment, I sat and read the newspaper, and then thought, Now what am I to do?"

When Robert moved out of his home, he knew that he would never return. He refers to his "mourning period" as beginning while he still lived there. Two of Lois's younger brothers had died separately and unexpectedly a few years after Robert and Lois were married. Robert identified the feelings that he had in the throes of separation as being similar to the grief cycle he watched members of Lois's family experience. He saw parallels between their stages of grief in accepting the boys' deaths, and his feeling of loss as he faced divorce. He drew solace in recognizing these similarities because they indicated to him that his decision to leave was not superficial, but of deep personal significance.

His bereavement was compounded by the guilt he felt for leaving both a sick woman, as well as his college-age children. "No matter their ages, it's difficult to leave children." His only confidant was a business associate, also an ordained minister, who had the special gift of being an impartial listener. At first, Robert spent weekends by himself, working on his motorboat, "sometimes from morning to night." But because his wife had rejected him for reasons that she never named, social acceptance became very important to him. He had been so accustomed to an isolated life, that he did not realize how much he had missed being with people. "I was really touched," he confided, "when old friends would see me in restaurants and tell me how good it was to see me out."

After a while, he struck up a relationship with a divorced woman who offered him sympathy and companionship. She was important to his regaining self-esteem. "We had fun," Robert remembered. "I was never in love with her, but she moved in. For a while it was an ideal relationship for both of us. Then we parted amicably."

Now after two years of being on his own, Robert is no longer ambivalent about wanting a divorce. When Lois asked for a separation, they did not know what they really wanted to achieve by living apart. Now Robert contends that separation in itself offers no cure for an ailing marriage. "We failed to discuss a time period or what we were trying to accomplish, except the hope that I would change the behavior that produced such anxiety for Lois. We never actually addressed the possibility of divorce face to face until last month. I finally said, 'You realize that this marriage is over and we should get a divorce.' Until then, Lois had been afraid to speak or hear those words, and I didn't want to upset her by bringing them up. But I knew when I left that I would never return. A separation doesn't remedy a thing. It only delays the inevitable and prevents a couple from moving on with their lives."

Robert's main regret was that he did not work toward achieving a more balanced relationship with Lois from the very beginning. From his perspective, low self-esteem plagued her to the degree that she wanted him to make all the decisions that affected them. If he questioned her passivity, she said she was too sick to become involved, causing Robert to back off. Robert praised Lois as a "good mother and attentive wife, but sacrificial to the point of ignoring her own needs.

"She had such low self-esteem that she wanted to do anything to please me. I didn't want that, but I went along in order, I thought, to keep her well. I pushed my own needs under the rug. What an irony! We were both experts at denial."

Robert Fenner did not want to reduce his wife to the lowest status of the second sex. But at great personal cost, Lois preferred to imitate the dependent role of her mother and continue the docile behavior that so pleased her father. Robert cannot be described as a feminist, but he appreciates how satisfying a marriage is when both partners recognize their equal worth. Robert is planning to marry a divorced woman who has long been on her own as a regional sales representative for a national line of cosmetics. Someone who obviously knows how to find her own way.

* * *

Myths are plentiful about male/female behavior that vanish in terms of real life. On the surface, Robert Fenner's rebounding from 26 years of a sad marriage to marry within a few years fulfills a belief that men quickly sail through divorce and into the arms of another woman. In reality, Robert's behavior runs counter to this stereotype. For years, he fulfilled his obligations to a sick wife who was never happy with him. He was devoted to her in the same way a long-suffering wife is dedicated to serving an ungrateful husband. He mourned the loss of his marriage long before the divorce occurred. Separation and divorce were most painful to him. His story disrupts a conventional truth that a man can always walk away from an unhappy marriage to a burdensome wife and sever his commitment without conscience.

Guilt and the Pain of Leaving

Our understanding of divorce is based on the situations of women. This bias may cause us to take the word of men less seriously. But their stories reveal how short-sighteded it is to adopt only a single perspective. To do so fails to adequately define divorce as a personal tragedy experienced by both partners. It trivializes marriage, and it risks suggesting to young men that they can enter into this institution with a cavalier spirit, for if all is not well, they can escape unscathed. The reality is that divorce is seldom an easy way for either men or women to put their marriages behind them.

Mark Keating, age 42, is another example of a man who struggled with his conscience and died a thousand times before making the decision to divorce his wife. After his separation, he truly epitomized a haunted man in spiritual crisis. For days at a time, he remained in a stoned and drunk state. He wryly referred to himself as "co-founder of the Neighborhood Drug and Alcohol Society; that means we were in favor of its use. We were a bunch of lost souls beat up from bad marriages. My house became a haven, a den of iniquity for us."

Once separated, Mark wanted to fall in love with the first woman he dated. "I wanted to be married so bad. But thank God she was smarter than I. She had a lot of the traits of my first wife, and I was accommodating them. The dressing was different, but she was the same woman. If we had married, I'd only be divorced again, or trying to figure out some way to escape." In mock sententious tones, he proclaimed: "My advice to the world is to find out who the hell you are after a divorce. Particularly if you were married young, you can get caught up in the day-to-day things and never discover your real potential or needs or expression."

A professional photographer, Mark found it hard to look at the stills he took in the last years of his marriage because they reflected such pain. "Most of them are lonely shots of dead trees or abandoned buildings. There's no life in them; no hope." Nevertheless, Mark called himself a "lucky son of a bitch," even though he now copes with multiple sclerosis, a disease often related to stress. His first symptoms also appeared in those final, worst days.

* * *

Mark gave his high school sweetheart, "the prettiest girl I ever met," an engagement ring when he was on a Navy furlough, and she was in nursing school. With some pride, he noted that he was the only "guy who didn't get a Dear John letter." Returning home, Mark started college on the G.I. bill, and married Jenny Stricker during his sophomore year.

"I thought I would be married forever," Mark measured his words, "so I didn't put a lot into the relationship. No matter what, I thought it would last. It was a different time. I didn't know any better."

With Jenny's salary, the G.I. bill, and Mark's part-time jobs in photography, the couple supported themselves. "Jenny was always the stable one. I was the wacko." Mark shook his head. She went to work every day. I tried it for nine months. After I dropped out of college in my senior year—one step short of flunking—I worked as a technical photographer. We bought a big, old house, then I went into business for myself, free-lancing. I knew I could never work for anybody. In the meantime, Jenny finished college."

A railroad buff from his boyhood days, Mark spent weekends taking pictures of trains. "Right now I have one of the best negative files on trains in the country, but Jenny resented the time I invested." Then the offer came for Mark's dream job: to be a freight expediter on the railroad. "There were only about 60 of us in the nation, and I was the youngest. An expediter is responsible for moving heavy equipment from a point of origin to its destination. It was a great chance for me to see the United States on an expense account and also to be with trains. I was paid by the trip on a day basis, so I could be at home as much as I wanted to be. Trips were anywhere from two days to a month, but the deal was you had to stay until the job was done. My average was ten days. The boss also insisted that I call home every night."

For one month, the Keatings enjoyed economic security. Mark was making money traveling on his dream railroad. Having finished her bachelor's degree in nursing, Jenny worked in a pediatric intensive care unit. But 30 days later, when Mark called Jenny to tell her that he had completed a job and was flying home, she startled him by saying that she had seen him that day in Boston Common. Troubled, Mark carefully explained that he was in Chicago. A neighbor met

Mark at Logan Airport, saying that Jenny was crying uncontrollably at home. Mark found her underneath a table, irrational and inconsolable, sobbing that everyone in her family had been killed. A psychiatrist admitted her to the mental health unit of a general hospital. After two weeks, Jenny was released.

Mark claimed that he did not know how to react to Jenny's illness. "I had never dealt with a mental problem before. We talk so easily about nervous breakdowns without knowing what that really means. I thought being in the hospital for a mental problem was the same as for a physical problem. That when you came out, you were okay. I really didn't understand that Jenny was stabilized by drugs. I didn't have any help in understanding that her condition was not an isolated problem. Either the support system wasn't there, or I didn't know how to use it."

Mark felt sure that Jenny's condition had been provoked by her having started a new job almost immediately after graduating from college. If they took a vacation together and if she left intensive-care nursing for floor duty, Mark was confident that the future would be brighter.

However, over the next three years, Jenny had four more breakdowns. Mark knew the signals. "Even her vocabulary would change. When I would hear her say certain things like, 'I see said the blind man, as he picked up his hammer and saw,' I would feel as if I had been pushed off an elevator shaft. I'd think, Oh, there you go. Nothing I can do except ride this out."

Mark and Jenny were married ten years when she was hospitalized for the fourth time. Her behavior became erratic while they were visiting Jenny's parents in Rhode Island. Mark recalled the scene: "For 24 hours she screamed and yelled in a hotel room. I tried to calm her down and talk her out of it. Sometimes I would be successful, but this time I wasn't. She directed everything at me, yelled and cursed about my job. I finally thought, If I'm the cause of all this pain, I quit."

Jenny's parents hospitalized her while Mark returned to Boston. Quietly, Mark explained, "I couldn't handle another breakdown. I knew that I had to save myself. I had to keep myself together. It didn't matter that I also felt as guilty as hell. I had a headache that lasted for three years. Then right after she left the hospital, Jenny hooked up with some guy and ended up as a bag lady in Providence. I tried to find her and put her into a hospital. She screamed and cursed at me, and I went back home. Only then did her father tell me that her mother had had similar problems. And he had stayed because of the children."

At first, Mark was euphoric to be free of his burden. "Then reality set in, and I realized I was going to be alone." After their divorce, Jenny married "a guy as down and out as she. It was something out of *Ironweed*, but they have helped each other to make a go of it."

Mark's rehabilitation was slow because of torturous guilt. "My friends would say that I had done everything possible, had stayed as long as I could. Then I would think, No, I could have stayed a little longer had I just put my mind to it. In all honesty, I knew better. But I couldn't stop thinking about the pain I had inflicted on Jenny by being on the road, by putting my interests first."

Separated a year, Mark had a catharsis with an old friend, a woman "whom I love dearly, always will. I got rip-roaring drunk and really let everything out. The next morning I had a glimmer that one of these days I was going to get better." His first positive step was to admit that he was tired of living and working alone. So he quit the railroad and returned to his Boston suburb to work as a free-lance photographer. Mark acknowledged, "Two other good things happened then that are still important to me. I started bike riding and taught myself to play the guitar." But Mark's recovery was never meteoric. He began a cycle of alcohol and substance abuse. It was during this time that his house also became the headquarters for the mock "Drinking and Alcohol Society."

One winter morning, after being stoned for 20 straight nights, Mark took a hard look at himself. "I knew that I was headed for disaster if I kept up that way. I helped myself to move away from drugs by selling the house. I felt that it was haunted, that Jenny was still there. I quit drinking easily enough and joined Adult Children of Alcoholics because I'm from an alcoholic family. The guys who used to drink and smoke at my house are now in AA or Al-Anon. Now we talk AA instead of booze."

In this transition stage, Mark also coped with acute physical changes. He claimed that he knew that he had multiple sclerosis even before hearing the medical diagnosis. He traced the start of his symptoms to the last year of his marriage, and explained how he knew.

"Jenny's medical books were still around. I narrowed my problem to a spinal tumor, MS, or a physical injury. In time, I didn't die of the tumor; I knew that I hadn't been injured, so I felt sure that I had MS because it is a disease associated with stress. A friend said, 'Oh you don't have that. But get it diagnosed.'" Mark waited until a lull in his photography business to see a physician, and responded in typical fashion to the official diagnosis by "getting real drunk for a week. Then I thought, Get on with it."

During the years that Mark "drank like hell," he also tried to keep physically fit by running and bicycling. He credited bicycling with the fact that he is even walking. But more than just exercise, bicycling became a ritual for Mark that defined his year and motivated him to live. Each summer, for example, he now plans a two-week biking trip where he rides 100 miles a day, "although the disease has slowed me down a bit."

Hearing Mark Keating talk about bicycling was almost like listening to a Walt Whitman poem: "Living on a bike is the most fantastic thing I can imagine. You are open to everything that comes along. You're part of everything that happens if you have a bicycle. I wake up at dawn and think, Let's get at it. Bicycling has made a huge difference in my life. It gives me a sense of accomplishment and well-being."

But no matter what gains he had made, Mark felt particularly alone when he turned 40. "I was self-pitying, not happy, down about my health. I wanted to sell everything and go out on my bicycle for a couple of years. My friends said, 'Look, we love you. Please stay.' It's always been all right for me to love people, but not the other way around. I think, Why in the hell would anyone want to love me?"

To answer that question, Mark bicycled by himself through the Northeast. "I decided that I was living with the people I wanted to be with, and doing the work that I wanted to do. I had the constancy and love of a family that I had created, not my family of origin. I know I won't end up old and alone. Being by myself on a bike helps me to figure things like that out. Bicycling contains everything I know about.

I love geography. I love the road. I love mechanics. I love geology. I look at the rocks when I'm out there. I look at nature. I look at old railroad yards and at canals. I'm part of the whole thing."

His exultant testimony continued. "I think of myself as an albatross, big and clumsy on the ground. My MS is active, I drag my left foot, have trouble climbing stairs. But get an albatross in the air, and it flies gracefully for thousands of miles. That's the way I am on a bicycle. As long as I can ride, I'll have a source of strength. I've been through a lot of shit, but I'm fortunate. Wow! I've made it. I'm still here. How about that?"

Mark's guitar is almost as important to him as his bicycle. "When I turn wacko, it helps me to play by myself, to hear my own voice singing words that are mine. It relieves my blues." Mark's songs have not been published, but his friends know the titles well: "Teaching Pigs to Sing" and "Put on Your Gray Suit for Jesus."

As he spoke about how closely his guitar was tuned to his own voice, Mark returned to the differences between him and Jenny. As one of six children, he was always trying to figure out a way to be alone. He craved and enjoyed solitude, which was why he was drawn to photography as a hobby. On the other hand, Jenny never lived by herself. She moved from her family house into a nursing school dormitory and then into a home with Mark, who soon took to the road.

"Some of these things we're talking about happened 14 years ago," Mark concluded, "but I still remember it chapter and verse. I can tell you what Jenny was wearing. Just talking makes me relive it. It's good for me to do that once in a while because scar tissue starts to build up. Being the husband of someone mentally ill was the hardest thing I've ever done. But I'm still here. I have talents and interests to draw on. I have a great library. I finally believe in my talents. Each day is different for me. I'm one tough son of a bitch, and I'm pretty lucky. . . . I want to show you the soles of my shoes. See how the left one is all worn? That's the way my leg drags."

* * *

Mark Keating knew that his story was not a model for how to achieve happiness after divorce. Nonetheless, his spiritual crisis followed the classic pattern of emergence from anxiety, despair, and chaos, toward the light of hope and affirmation. He made the long journey by trusting friends, making life-giving choices, maintaining a sense of humor, and adopting an athletic hobby that he loved.

The best way for ex-husbands to acquire Mark's inner peace is to probe for answers in the existing circumstances of their own lives. By contrast, Dan Nicholson, the president of a small accounting firm, told why he wears a medical alert bracelet engraved, "Do not resuscitate."

"I have no great interest in putting up with my life longer than I have to. Life is nothing that I value. Obviously, I wish I had never married Karen. But if you do one thing different, then everything else changes. Who knows? I may have done worse. There's the old saying that we choose our own poison."

Yet Dan referred to the words from the Anglican wedding liturgy that marriage is ordained for the "mutual aid and comfort of the married couple" as describing his own ideal. Little about his 15-year marriage offered him solace and succor, however.

Beyond Belief: A Battered Husband

Dan Nicholson called himself a "battered husband." He was willing to be interviewed because public awareness of physically abused men is minimal and unsympathetic. Battered men have been a laughing matter from the time of Aristophanes. Henpecked husbands and shrewish wives prevail in early English comedy and call to mind the Wife of Bath. In popular culture, cartoons of Maggie chasing Jiggs with her rolling pin are indelible in the national imagination. But husband-battering is a serious issue, as Dan Nicholson and other men in similar circumstances know.

Dan drew poignant analogies between the morbidity of physically abused men and the post-traumatic stress experienced by Vietnam veterans. "Violence does its physical damage, but the lack of social support is really what kills us," Dan pointed out. "When an abused man reveals his situation, he only experiences more punishment and derision from a society that sees his position as unacceptable."

The happiest times in Dan and Karen Nicholson's relationship were the months they lived together before they were even an official couple. Dan and Karen became friends when he was employed in the treasurer's office of the university where she was a senior majoring in Spanish. Karen often complained to Dan about living conditions in the dorm, so when he moved into a large apartment, he offered her a room. Within a few weeks, they were sleeping together. That summer, only months before their wedding, Dan had his first insight into Karen's dependency on him when she enrolled in a language institute at Middlebury College. Her first night on campus she called him at eleven o'clock so he could "rescue" her from an anxiety attack.

Dan immediately hopped into the car and drove six straight hours to comfort her. He marked this as the beginning of his recognition of their codependency. He pointed out that Karen's reliance on him grew stronger when she was hired by a secondary school to teach modern languages. Her self-confidence with other faculty members was so low that she rehearsed conversations with Dan before attending school functions. After faculty parties, she would review every minute of the evening to see "how I thought she was scoring. She expected me to be omniscient and omnipotent. I was expected to be able to tell her how to conduct herself in society, how to be successful and admired. Yet at the same time, she would tell me what a failure I was at my job. I put up with this because I felt it was my duty."

In the meantime, Karen went from therapist to therapist in the hopes of elevating her self-esteem. Her verbal abuse escalated after one of them encouraged her to express her emotions more freely. This permission resulted in what Dan described as a vituperative attack on him that lasted for three days. When he told her, "I have a right to express my feelings, too," Karen lurched after him. Dan claims that their marriage remained on keel as long as he assumed "responsibility for everything in and out of bed and expected nothing from her. It was a matter of gender stereotyping. I felt guilt that our problems were all my fault. It took me awhile to get over that." Ironically, the marriage also sailed on an even course until he stopped drinking. Dan marked the start of Karen's physical abuse with his turning away from alcohol. "My drinking," Dan analyzed, "provided her a very satisfying and covert way of practicing martyrdom. She could be self-destructive without the obvious dynamics."

Karen began hitting, slapping, choking, kicking, and gouging after Dan started transcendental meditation and mastered his need for drinking and smoking. "I developed more common sense," Dan explained, "and began to think more clearly. I was no longer willing to cooperate with the destructive patterns we had developed. We could have kept up our behavior until I died if I had continued to take total responsibility as parent, scapegoat, and provider."

Dan concluded that his decision to stop drinking became a "control issue" with Karen that inspired her violence. He described her as "spending life in a panic. She had a terrible self-image, absolutely no self-esteem. The fact that she was able to abuse me represented safety for her. She could never be so bad that I would abandon her." Dan noted that abused husbands or wives are most vulnerable to being brutalized when they reach the point of saying "never again." In his case, Karen's violence became uncontrollable when she feared losing control over *him*.

At first, Dan tried to protect himself by grabbing her arms. He clearly remembered the moment he made a conscious decision to never retaliate. "I raised my hand to strike back and saw a mask of erotic excitement on Karen's face. I became as disgusted with my own behavior as I was with hers. When I dropped my hand, her expression changed to sheer terror because, as I interpret, she was losing more control."

After that incident, Karen's behavior became more unpredictable. Assaults were random and could spring from verbal arguments or Karen's bad moods. Dan began to sleep in his clothes, protected by a locked bedroom door. But Karen would sit against the wall, talking to him for hours. If he tried to leave, she would grab his throat. Because of his sleeplessness, Dan's small accounting and tax business began to suffer.

Dan explained that physical retaliation is not a realistic option for a husband when he is being attacked by his wife. "It's dangerous for a man to defend himself," he says, "because then he's charged as the abuser. The man is generally stronger and can cause serious physical damage. Who believes him that he's acting in self-defense? Then what exactly are you going to do after restraining her? You can hardly tie her up!"

Dan continued to withstand Karen's punching and slapping. On one occasion, he hit his head against a tile bathtub after being pushed forward. When he was wearing a nose guard after surgery, she punched him and opened the stitches. The night Dan talked seriously to Karen about separating, she locked her arms around his throat from behind, pulling him to the floor. Afraid for his life, Dan reached for the phone to call the police. But Karen knocked it out of his hand and repeatedly struck him with the receiver. Later, she explained that she was terrified that she would have been institutionalized.

After escaping from the house, Dan called the police from a public telephone. The officer on duty persuaded him that the marriage would probably not survive if he filed charges. And Dan still held out hope. Within the week, the policeman returned to their home and tried to persuade Karen to seek counseling. "His follow-up was effective," Dan said, "because Karen saw a new therapist and seemed to make an effort for a few weeks. Yet, her behavior ultimately did not change. Always at the point in therapy where it was time for some self-confrontation, Karen would leave."

Nonetheless, Karen was eager to prove her growing sense of independence and did not object when Dan had to leave on a business trip. But driving him to the airport, she began crying and weaving dangerously across the highway. Dan managed to have her pull the car over to the side of the road, and he took the keys. It was a tough choice to decide between taking her to the emergency room of a hospital or driving to the airport, but he chose to go on with his trip on the basis that, with all of her histrionics, Karen had never hurt herself. Dan checked in at curbside and sent Karen on her way. Yet five years later, he still wonders if he made the right decision. "At that time I wanted to avoid her deepest fear of being institutionalized. Maybe I shouldn't have been so concerned about that."

The problems in Dan's domestic life were compounded because he and Karen worked together in their accounting business, where she became a "loose cannon. Karen wouldn't let me out of her sight. Once she walked into the room when I was holding a seminar for owners of small businesses on how to transfer their financial records to computers. Karen sat on the desk behind me, swinging her legs like a metronome. I never knew what to expect from her. The tension became more and more difficult. After sleepless nights and fear of these kinds of surprises, I couldn't produce."

When we spoke, Dan had been divorced from Karen for five years, but he claimed that the damage from their marriage was unalterable. The first time he saw Karen after their divorce, he had to pull the car to the side of the road and vomit. Recently, he saw her again and was only mildly depressed for a few days, but Dan has developed a number of physical ailments that he attributes to his years of living with stress. Although he has many friends who are women, he has few thoughts about marrying again. One of them invited Dan to lunch during his divorce and said, "You must hate women."

Dan responded to that comment through analogy. "During college I had a black roommate. After I got to know him well, he said, 'I don't hate white people, but I watch them for a long, long time. I don't care how good a liberal line they talk, I watch them for a long time before I know where I'm going to take my chances with them.'"

Dan concluded, "I'm watchful with women I don't know yet, but that's not misogyny. It's hard for me to get myself back to the point where I can trust physical intimacy. It's not a high priority with me now."

Dan made the distinction that for him, emotional pain was the worst part of absorbing physical abuse because he had always been demonstrably affectionate. "I always sat on the same side of the restaurant booth or table and always had an arm around Karen." His voice tightening, Dan went on. "What was extraordinarily painful for me as things got bad was the conflict between the demand that I be intimate, and the knowledge that my intimacy would be betrayed. Consequently, the chronic experience of betrayal and intimacy was the worst for me. In the end, maybe men are more thin-skinned about emotional relationships than women are. I think machismo can be a defensive reaction to how badly men can be hurt. When a woman starts saying that we should be more open and vulnerable, I think of Lucy holding the football for Charlie Brown."

Since his divorce, Dan has been dedicated to bringing public attention to the complexities of domestic violence. He works for many organizations that support human justice causes. His strongest legacy, however, is given to the young men he speaks with in college and high school workshops on gender issues. His basic message is that men have a shared investment in alleviating the suppression of women, for then they will also liberate themselves from assuming total responsibility in their private relationships. Through practical examples and role-playing, he urges young men to see how they are susceptible to manipulation when women do not exercise their power to choose and make decisions. The message on Dan Nicholson's medical bracelet asks that he not be resuscitated in an emergency. But this does not mean that he has lost faith in a better life for others.

* * *

Long-suffering men talk openly about their feelings after they have descended into their grief, mourned the past, and then released it. Contrary to how we might expect ex-husbands to respond, they do not hide from describing their psychic pain and secrets of abuse. They speak plainly about their failings, and they struggle to exorcise demons of guilt. They reveal themselves through workaday images of itchy shirts, old railroad yards, shipshape motorboats, and even medical bracelets of flinty steel. Their stages of recovery range between joyful celebration to a tentative acceptance of the way things really are. They represent a divergent view on the stereotype that a long-suffering spouse must be a saintly woman.

COMFORTABLE
INCOMPATIBILITY

What we call the beginning is often the end
And to make an end is to make a beginning.

from *Little Gidding,* by T. S. Eliot

PUBLIC SYMPATHY FOR the individuals involved in incompatible marriages is generally reserved for women presumed to be locked into this type of situation due to a lack of career options and economic insecurity. The truth is that men also have unique pressures that force them to continue to live in comfortable incompatibility.

At best, marriage is a self-conscious effort for husbands who sense that the relationship with their wives ought to be more than what it is. Yet, they will not risk the upheaval that might result from changing what it is that they cannot even name. In some cases, men resist admitting that time-honored definitions of the ideal husband are actually self-destructive. The mark of a "good husband" has long been the stoical ability to curb the expression of his own emotional and spiritual needs in order to provide for the welfare of wife and children. As breadwinner, he takes to heart that his first responsibility is to ensure the comfort of his family. Marriage is serious business, and "real" men carry the burden and the guilt.

Classic cases of incompatibility encompass the stories of husbands who are blind to their wives' unhappiness. Increasingly, this scenario refers to men who assume that the new climate for women has been breezing right past their own homes. Even when change occurs before their very eyes, husbands will not see wives charting new goals or hear them reevaluating the terms of their marriage. These men have yet to ponder the effect that developing opportunities for women have on the dynamics of their own personal lives. But their hurt is no less real than their shock when forced to face what they never thought could happen to them.

Whatever the issue of the resisting husband in an incompatible marriage, the problem is plain: No matter how promising a marriage may seem at first, emotional growth and mutual understanding must evolve if a couple is to work through the inevitable changes in their tastes and values. If not, husbands and wives will live out their days in comfortable incompatibility, accepting or denying the way things are or seem to have to be. However, an unexpected experience often provokes such eye-opening insight that even a resigned husband will confront the reality that he and his wife have grown far apart.

A Good Husband Expects Little

Ben Lefton recalled such a turning point when he visited Israel with his wife—a trip that was the fulfillment of a lifelong dream for him. "For Audrey, Israel was a shopping spree. She went from kiosk to kiosk looking for the latest in Israeli jewelry. I was overwhelmed by my heritage, by the Holocaust. In fact, I was bitter. But Audrey was almost flippant. We visited a kibbutz on the Golan Heights. This was right after the 12-Day War, so it was basically under siege. The women had a hard life taking care of the children, holding things together while the men farmed.

A very hardworking man remarked, 'Life here is as hard as hell,' and he gestured to the earth to show how thin it was. During all of this, a tourist next to me kept filing her nails, and then suddenly exploded, 'Goddamn it, I broke my nail.' It was something out of a Woody Allen movie. Later, when I tried to talk about what happened, Audrey didn't understand why I was so upset. 'So what's the matter? She broke her nail,' she said. For Audrey, our trip to Israel wasn't any different than going to the Bahamas. I grew very resentful of her values."

While they were in the Golan Heights, Ben finally realized what had he had not acknowledged before: When it came to the most important values in life, he and Audrey had divergent views. Even with marriage counseling, they were never able to discuss their problems with each other because they could never agree on what their problems were. "We simply looked at life in different ways," Ben shrugged, "and had no basis for communication."

Ben was puzzled when questioned about his expectations of marriage, but finally admitted, "Zero. By today's standards and based on what I know now, that's bizarre. But I got married to be like everybody else. It was the logical thing to do, and the outcome was a family."

Ben linked his passive attitude toward marriage to his growing up male in our post-World War II society. Until adolescence, girls were excluded from his experiences of male camaraderie. Looking back, he acknowledges that he never knew how to talk to a young woman. "I never considered that a woman could be a good friend or a companion. Women were always a mystery or the enemy." He married without recognizing any need for a feminine confidante.

Ben was never happy in his marriage, but did not know what needed to be changed. He apologized for using an analogy: "During the night, if you find mosquitoes biting you, you keep swatting them away. But the real problem is that you forgot to close the window. I didn't know that the window was open. I was only swatting the bugs, but so was Audrey. Neither one of us understood enough to know where to start."

His own father, a credit manager for an independently owned furniture company, earned enough to support Ben, an only child, and his wife, who stayed at home. Their relationship became a model for Ben's idea of marriage. "Mother was always there, putting breakfast and dinner on the table, and my father provided. Home was a haven for him. That was expected. And, as far as I could see, that's what marriage was about."

By comparison, Ben never felt that Audrey made a home for him. "I sensed I was working for my wife. I was her employee," he clarified. "If she wanted some material object, her message was, 'Well, Jewish men provide. They do it because they do it.' I was enraged by the idea that something was always expected of me. Audrey did not assume any responsibility, even for mailing the monthly bills or keeping track of our checking account. I would come home at night to more work and aggravation. The message was 'Jewish men have to make life free and easy so that we can run around and have lunch with our sisters.' I bitterly resented it. I felt I was being used. I got nothing in return. Audrey's position was, 'I'm the wife. I had the children. I'm done now.' I just didn't get any nourishment from my marriage."

An electrical engineer, Ben owns a flourishing industrial and commercial building supply company located in a small New Jersey town, where Audrey's parents and three married sisters also live. Even as newlyweds, Ben never felt he was the focus of his wife's love, but that her parents and sisters always came first. "The biggest decision of Audrey's day was where she and her sisters would meet for lunch. Their phone calls would start at 10:00 A.M. Nothing between Audrey and me was sacred. She discussed everything, I mean everything, with her sisters. I still keep in touch with a brother-in-law, who also recently divorced, and he agreed that there were no secrets among the sisters."

Ben never felt at home in his marriage, but that fact did not make him feel less guilty about not making Audrey happy. A good sex life was always their bromide. But in 1982, after a Caribbean cruise, they decided that a physical separation might help them to reunite. For two years, Audrey lived in Fort Lauderdale, where her parents had retired, but the distance helped to convince Ben that "we simply did not nourish each other. But I still saw our problems as essentially my fault. I kept dwelling on what I hadn't accomplished, and that included not making my wife happy."

When Audrey returned to New Jersey, she and Ben lived apart for two more years, leading very independent lives. Ben was despondent, nonetheless, because he had such a negative self-concept and suffered such shame because of his perceived failure as a husband. Friends encouraged him to attend an intensive three-day weekend seminar on healing and developing self-esteem sponsored by the Omega Institute for Holistic Studies in Rhinebeck, New York. It helped him to see that he had been assuming the entire responsibility for the unraveling of his marriage. His marriage defined his identity, even though he and Audrey had lived separately for a number of years. All in all, Ben felt second-rate.

While participating in the seminar, Ben was encouraged to express his values with confidence. Ben described the experience as a "tremendous breakthrough in my perception of myself. It helped me to understand what I admired in people and didn't admire, and why I enjoyed some people and not others. It helped me to dwell on my accomplishments in life, and to put my failures in perspective."

In the final session, Ben heard himself speak for the first time about the incident on the Golan Heights, and admitted to himself that it revealed the basic differences between him and Audrey. Only then did Ben feel psychologically liberated to end his marriage. "This probably sounds simplistic," he reflected, "but the person most difficult to tell the truth to is yourself."

Divorced five years, Ben will soon marry an attorney, a woman who finished law school after her own divorce as a young mother with three children. It matters to Ben that she is loyal to her Jewish heritage and responsible about her parents. "But I know her first commitment will be to me. I feel protected in her company. If I'm tired, she's concerned. If I have a problem, we can talk about it. We share each other's day. We can also have objective discussions about what's going on in the world.

"I never knew it was possible to talk to a woman like this. It's important to me that besides everything else, she's my trusted friend. I grew up with such macho stereotypes that it never occurred to me that a woman could write a book or practice law or even be interested in my work. And I'm very happy."

Ben felt the relief inherent in openly expressing his feelings. He welcomed the chance to liberate himself from cultural stereotypes that required good husbands to be ultimately responsive to their wives' comfort while expecting little sensitivity in return. Over the years, Ben felt guilty if he brooded about these unreasonable expectations. His desire to have deeper bonds with his wife seemed "soft" and unmanly. After all, his own father protected their home without feeling distressed that he was not sharing, communicating, listening, and responding to his wife and son. By accepting his father's example, Ben denied himself the friendship of women, and married to be in service.

* * *

One of the most difficult truths for men to see is that blind loyalty to patriarchal tradition ultimately thwarts their own self-definition. On the other hand, men who do not want to clone the driven breadwinners of the past have few opportunities for exploring ways of breaking out of gender stereotypes. Men's groups are springing up across the country discussing issues that affect every aspect of how men experience their lives as boys, sons, fathers, brothers, friends, lovers, and husbands. But only a small percentage of American men are taking advantage of them.

There is a tendency to say that men's lives are changing dramatically, but my interviews seem to suggest only that men do not want to act the way they always have, or the way they have always been expected to act. They want to explore broader options as loving fathers, enhance their communication with women, and have more flexibility when it comes to balancing family and career. The '90s challenge is for men to find comfortable ways of facing these issues in a variety of forums, without feeling that they are becoming feminized.

Never a Talker

When he married at age 25, Joe Graciano, like Ben Lefton, failed to understand that the real test of masculine maturity is not in marriage itself, but in the willingness to grow together with a spouse, who will also act sensitively and responsibly toward him.

In 1967, Joe married Joann Indovina, the first girl he had ever really dated. She was a waitress in a trattoria owned by her uncle, a mutual friend of Joe's close buddy. They shared strong ethnic ties, and the relationship seemed safe. Even at the time of our conversation, Joe couldn't say what he had wanted his marriage to be. He only knew that young men were expected to marry and settle down shortly after college.

When he referred to his marriage, Joe remarked, "I guess there were no high points, nothing ever really good about it." Yet Joe, newly divorced, wept about his loss, saying that he felt "detached, as if I'm on TV, that I'm not living a real life anymore."

Married barely a year when their cedar home burned to the ground, Joe and Joann moved in with his widowed father in order to save money. Unfortunately, Joe's father resented Joann because her parents were from a different region of Italy than he. Joann tried to avoid the tension when she left each day for work in a city office, but Joe admitted that it was difficult for him to listen to Joann's descriptions of his father's criticism of her. In the evening, Joann looked forward to escaping from her father-in-law's kitchen by driving down the hill to meet Joe at the bus stop. But one night when he arrived home before she did, he did not meet *her* at the bus stop, but instead, stayed home and talked to his father. Twenty years later, Joann brought this hurtful slight to his attention.

"Every time we talk, she tells me how hard my father was on her. How she packed my lunch and had to act like my mother. But I never asked her to do those things." Joe burst into heartfelt tears.

As a result of fertility problems, Joann continued working as a secretary for eight years before having two children. "We needed money, and there was no reason for her to just take care of the house," Joe apologized. Their financial status improved in the next ten years, however, as Joe progressed through middle management in a growing corporation. But bills also piled up because Joann's spending escalated with Joe's salary. Consequently, he took out a home equity loan, using two-thirds of it to pay old debts.

For a fresh start, he turned over the household accounts to Joann, hoping that she would become more aware of expenses. Joann reported that bookkeeping was easy and wondered why Joe had made such a fuss. Initially impressed by the way she balanced the budget, he soon discovered that she was using the remaining third of the loan for shopping sprees. Joe said, "I went crazy. Joann was making good money as a country club waitress, but she also bought an expensive outfit every week."

Joe saw Joann's spending solely as an economic problem, not as a symptom of her unspoken emotional needs. "We just never talked about how we really felt. We just went from day to day." So through it all, Joe never thought his marriage was in trouble. When Joann lingered after hours at the country club, kibbitzing with the dining room staff, Joe was slow to verbalize his hurt that she was never able to stay up so late with *him*. "At home, she would be in bed by eight o'clock."

With hindsight, Joe saw the results of "never being a talker. Now

I know that I took my anger out on the kids, always telling them to be quiet and go to their rooms. Instead of Joann and I screaming at each other, we'd yell at them. Joann and I seldom argued. Until she said she wanted a divorce, I never thought that we were unhappy."

Joe also distracted himself from his tattered marriage by working on his house, an old homestead that was "a disaster. Every minute of every day it required attention. Everything went wrong with it. We even lived in it while the kitchen was rebuilt. When it rained, the basement would flood. I was always cleaning out sewers and drains. It was a disaster on the marriage because I didn't handle these crises very well. But on the other hand, they kept us fighting about the house instead of with each other."

When they lived with his father as newlyweds, Joe and Joann learned to bottle up their feelings. Later, they dealt with their anger by diffusing it on house and children. Without having to admit it, the Gracianos grew further apart. Their sex life continued, "but not like it was when we were younger." Joe shook his head. During their last five years together, Joe never dreamed that Joann was preparing for divorce by becoming financially independent. She left the country club to join a hotel chain, where her management skills earned her a position in marketing and sales. Joe remembered his hurt when Joann finally talked about a divorce. "I said, 'You'll never find anyone as nice as me.'"

Joe admitted pleading and begging for another chance, even offering to see a marriage counselor. "But Joann said that I was too late. That I didn't listen when she wanted me to go." Joe stayed in the house as long as he could, then moved into an apartment.

For six months, Joe had weekly counseling sessions with a psychologist "who did not help, probably because I didn't want him to." But he did find companionship with a woman "just to go out." Hearing about Joe's new relationship, Joann accused him of betraying their intimate secrets. Moreover, she was angry that he had filed an extension on their income tax return. When Joe explained that he had a hard time focusing his mind to complete it on time, Joann yelled, "You can spend the rest of your life in jail for all I care." Within hours, she apologized and asked Joe to return home. "But so many things had been said that I couldn't put behind me." Joe tearfully explained that he waited for a few days before moving in with Joann.

Joe felt cramped living in Joann's new townhouse. He could not turn up the stereo because of the neighbors, and true to their style, the Gracianos never raised their own voices either. Yet, after a few months together, Joann said, "I feel absolutely nothing for you." His pride at stake, Joe called it quits.

Newly divorced, Joe did not understand why his wife wanted to be rid of him. With tears streaming down his face, he described his single life as "disgusting." Night after night, after leaving his office, Joe sat at the bar at a local motel, ate something, and then returned to his apartment for the eleven o'clock news. Once a week he visited with his children, but he dreaded that he might run into Joann's new boyfriend. "But even worse than that, I don't feel like a father anymore, picking up the kids for a few hours and dropping them off." Shared custody was never a possibility for Joe because "I never really entered into the divorce proceedings. I kept denying it was really taking place. I thought it would all go away." Now he regrets that.

Joe even gave up coaching his sons' baseball and soccer teams. "Joann sparkles so at games that I can't stand to go. She's always up, bubbly. That eats at me. She's so up and I'm so sad." Joe has yet to recognize that his behavior penalizes only himself and his relationship with his sons.

Joe has seized few opportunities to be introspective. But at least he knows that he is not yet dead. He thinks fleetingly about buying a home "where the kids would be comfortable to visit. I'm handy, and my older son has some ability with carpentry work. Maybe that would give us something to do together." But when a father expresses his anger about an unhappy marriage by punishing his sons, it is a real stretch when he needs them as an anchor.

After his marriage failed, Joe realized that he missed the old, demanding homestead and the grass he enjoyed mowing twice a week. "My wife accused me of using it as an excuse to be away from her and the boys." Unsure of himself, Joe muttered, "I just liked the exercise."

"Never much of a talker," Joe saw his divorce as his own personal failure. His consuming sadness was not tempered by any trust in his past behavior nor realistic judgment about his wife's demands. "We should have gone out to dinner more, talked. We always took camping and fishing trips. She didn't like them. I always thought she did."

Joann baffles him as much today as she did when confiding how lonely she felt as a bride living in his father's house. Joe continues to have little insight into her feelings or his own. Yet during our interview, Joe wept copiously. He saw no cure for his situation. He did not think that psychological help or more involvement with his children would bring him through.

The failure of his marriage cast a dark shadow over every aspect of Joe's life. He was filled with self-doubt and kept asking, "What's wrong with me?" He was in obvious pain, but would make no effort to repair himself. Sitting at a bar night after night certainly did little to help alleviate his depression.

Until Joe finds a center to his life, through whatever means, he will not have any peace. He cannot identify any bright moments in his past that could inspire his future. He is about to give up on himself. Nevertheless, while his marriage unraveled before his eyes, Joe acted as if it were strong enough to survive eternity. Indeed, the myth dies hard that all marriages are made in heaven, instead of by the choices people fail to make.

A Father's New Perspective

Rather than withdraw into fragile silences, husbands such as Joe Graciano would learn more about their incompatible marriages if they talked to their wives as passionate friends—like Monday-morning quarterbacks second-guessing the mistakes of Sunday's big game.

Yet, men may not share their personal concerns with their friends any more than they do with their wives. During our interview, a corporate executive wondered about the fact that he has eaten lunch with the same men for the past 20 years, but they know little about each others' private lives. "We talk about politics, football, restaurants. I can't say that we all really know each other the way women friends do." But since his divorce, Gene Baker claimed to be practicing his ability to listen, interact, and open up about himself. Then, he suddenly swung around in his leather chair and proudly gestured to the skyline of the city. "Just look at what a male value system gave us. That city wasn't built from feminine virtues. And now women want in on it. Things will change for the better when women get involved, but in the meantime, how do men adjust?" His attitude recalled Huckleberry Finn's accurate description of ambivalence when he felt "pretty comfortable all down one side, and pretty uncomfortable all up the other."

Gene was drawn to Marilyn Mott, his second wife, because of her "take-charge attitude and independent spirit. She was president of our local civic association. When I saw her in action, I thought, Now why couldn't I have married someone like that?" Gene's first marriage ended in divorce when his wife decided to return to her small Midwestern town rather than deal with the demands of her husband's climb to success, which left her feeling lonely.

Therefore, Gene appreciated Marilyn's stamina and ability to "get involved" while living on welfare as the divorced mother of two little boys. "We fell in love. We got married." Gene paused. "We were both very vulnerable. She was beautiful and interesting." Also, Marilyn was an army brat who would not resist moving when Gene decided that a change would boost his career.

Marilyn and Gene wanted to have a child, but after a miscarriage, doctors advised that another pregnancy would be risky. Gene traced the beginning of their problems to his adoption of Marilyn's two young sons, now college students. Immediately they had different ideas of how to be parents. "We had the same values, but not the same priorities. It was a matter of style," Gene concluded. "Things I did ten years ago are the tremendous obstacles that brought us to where we are today."

Applying the vocabulary of a management consultant to parenting skills, Gene described himself as being "results oriented" while Marilyn was "process oriented." She was patient and flexible with the children, while he was impatient and authoritarian. "I wanted them to be hard-driving, ambitious, and competitive." Gene cleared his throat. "Marilyn's main goal was for them to have good relationships with people, to be caring individuals. Looking back, I can see that I was autocratic and abusive in many respects. I would not find my behavior acceptable today. I wasn't at all democratic, but that's how I was raised."

The recent crisis in his marriage spurred Gene to reflect on his own childhood. "My parents were married for 50 years, but it was not a good marriage. They adapted to each other's habits. My father was an alcoholic. He had no idea about how to be a parent. My mother had only a third grade education, but she successfully ran a small business and was totally committed to the children. Just in the last six months, I had the insight that I had adopted my father's patterns, not my mother's. But my mother always took the rap when things didn't go right."

Gene was never a good listener with his wife or children. He agreed with Marilyn that this flaw was basic to their growing estrangement. Now he tries to do better. Instead of having one-way, finger-waving conversations with his sons and discrediting their opinions, he asks them questions.

"My sons say I'm a better guy than I was a year ago. I ask them how they feel about things, about their classes, and new experiences. We sometimes talk for a long time. I try not to have so much to say about myself. I shut up. Because I didn't do this before didn't mean I didn't care. I keep trying to persuade Marilyn to come back, to tell her that I'm a changed guy, but she won't."

Marilyn's apparently sudden decision to leave him a year ago still puzzled Gene. "Eight years ago," he explained, "she said she wanted a divorce but never acted on it. For a while, we were in counseling with a rinky-dink social worker who couldn't deal with my dominant personality. But I really don't know what suddenly triggered her after all these years to leave." In the meantime, Marilyn found a position earning $16,000 a year with a social service agency for worldwide humanitarian causes.

Marilyn told Gene that when she was on a flight from Africa, a "shadow suddenly came over her. That when she got home she knew she had to tell me that she couldn't continue to live with me. I thought divorce was ridiculous. We are both passionate, intense, stubborn people. That's what drew us together and made us compatible. I wanted to do everything possible and started counseling. Now I'm so changed. My aim through counseling was reconciliation. I wanted to maintain our commitment, but Marilyn didn't want to hear any of that. She felt she had done everything she could to keep the marriage together. In the last seven months, I felt the same about myself. But Marilyn didn't want to straighten it out anymore."

Gene figured that Marilyn gained confidence and "control of her life" by working. But he also counted on the fact that $16,000 a year is not an adequate safety net for her. "Hell, I met Marilyn by saving her. I must have had a tremendous need to save her and the kids." Gene shook his head in wonder.

The boys live with Gene because Marilyn moved from the house and can afford only an efficiency apartment. "It was her idea for a divorce," Gene insisted, "so why would I move from the house? I've changed. The boys and I have a tight relationship now. But Marilyn doesn't see any of my redeeming qualities. I've learned to integrate into my personality Marilyn's better qualities. I listen. I engage people more. I learned to do this from Marilyn. But I don't want to lose what I have that got me where I am today. I've achieved and accomplished."

When asked what he would do if he were to replay his life, Gene did not know what he could actually change. Even though Marilyn thought he devoted too many hours to working, Gene said that his career would still be the focus of his life. He explained that Marilyn's expectations were different because "marriage was the whole of her life."

Gene punched his desk. "But I can't do a hell of a lot of things well at the same time. I do what I can do. For example, if I play golf, I want to do it well. If I camp, I don't want to be in the woods just over-night. So marriage wasn't the most important part of my life. I set out to get ahead. That was my priority. It requires incredible energy. Life in the high-powered business world is a parade—the marchers, the actors, the process is constantly changing. The parade's always moving somewhere. You can't be alert and responsive to this and have a marriage and a relationship with a wife as central to your purpose. There should be a way to have both, but I don't know how it's done."

As Gene saw it, one of the advantages of having women in the work-place is that they will "come to understand the pressures men shoulder. They will become more like men and place less importance on marriage." Then Gene shifted into his ambivalent mode, pointing out that as women gain power, social institutions will change for the better, "will make us different people, but it's going to be hell getting there."

Ultimately, Gene exonerated himself and blamed Marilyn for their breaking up because she was not willing to "work through to salvage our commitment. Commitments are important to me. I never cheated on my wife. I lived intentionally in terms of a code. But I made a mistake. I believed I married somebody who had the same commitment as I. But after 15 years, she packed it in and walked away."

Nevertheless, to this day, Gene still dreams about Marilyn. "I know I can't continue to live with the pain that I feel. It's overwhelming at times. But I'm going to be all right. There were times when I couldn't imagine ever saying that."

Admitting vulnerability was a new experience for Gene. He could never risk missing a beat in the big parade by stopping to listen to the feelings of his wife, sons, friends, or even to express his own. But now Gene has an ambiguous sense of an evolving new man. He tells his sons, for example, that "they must recognize the importance of relationships, and that intimacy should be a part of their day-to-day style." With that conviction, Gene provides a legacy for his sons that he was not heir to from his father. And for now, that is brand-new territory as Gene begins to challenge the patriarchal assumptions that had always guided his life. Sadly, his efforts to save his sons came far too late to save his marriage.

* * *

It is difficult for men who have lived out traditional male roles in their marriages to change their old ways of relating to women at home and in the office. They may even feel more comfortable enduring incompatible marriages than raising questions with their wives for which there are no answers—and no turning back. Society has succeeded so well in supporting separate values for men and women that the husband who yearns to be more nurtured and nurturing pays no less an emotional price than the wife who seeks independence. The husband who lives by the rules of competition is no less thwarted than the woman who is denied self-expression. But until these contradictions are better resolved, incompatible unions will continue to be havens of paradoxical comfort for the Gene Bakers who choose to delay the moment of self-recognition until it is too late.

Husbands will deny that they and their wives are incompatible rather than risk making that decisive move that might lose the marriage for them. In this way, men are no different from women. Both husbands and wives choose to ignore problems rather than challenge the behavior and values that they had once accepted. At the time of their wedding, their choice of a spouse may have corresponded to their notion of what a marriage ought to be like, according to gender roles they had witnessed with their mothers and fathers.

In the past 30 years, women have grown accustomed to naming the oppression in their lives. On the other hand, men are just beginning to face the restrictions placed on them by a surface masculinity that favors separateness, stoicism, and competitiveness. The credo of the good father, "providing for others at one's own expense," has paradoxically resulted in husbands distancing themselves from the intimacy of family life. The current crisis for men obliges them to see that a narrow understanding of the role of provider limits their opportunities as nurturer, critically affecting their emotional relationships with wives, children, and themselves. Men are just beginning to assess what masculinity means in its deepest sense. To challenge the expression of husband and father as they have known it to be in the past is a painful process for them. But in rejecting the opportunity, they also sacrifice the joy of developing a personal and loving expression of marriage with their wives. The rewards are held at bay for couples who continue to live unhappily rather than to rewrite a script that fits themselves. The prolonged tension of living in comfortable incompatibility finally results in a separateness bridged by no false solutions—only divorce.

TIME BOMB

*. . . at some brighter period when the world
should have grown ripe for it, in Heaven's own
time a new truth would be revealed, in order to
establish the whole relation between man and
woman on a surer ground of mutual happiness.*

from *The Scarlet Letter,*
by Nathaniel Hawthorne

EVEN AFTER THREE DECADES, the news of women's liberation has
the power of affecting marriages as if Betty Friedan's *The Feminine
Mystique* were published only yesterday. Friedan's research revealed
the role of mother to be so idealized after World War II that only with
guilt could women pursue any employment, social cause, or intellectual satisfaction outside of the home until after children had "left the
nest." Wives wanting an identity other than child care provider and
housewife risked strong criticism.

The growing separation between the world of men and women was
further captured in Marilyn French's landmark novel *The Women's
Room.* More recent books such as Naomi Wolf's *Fire With Fire: The
New Female Power and How It Will Change the 21st Century,* and
Susan Faludi's *Backlash: The Undeclared War Against American
Women,* raise controversial questions about a "gender war" provoked
by sexual harassment, date rape, and images of female beauty created
by the media.

Wolf and Faludi, among others, are concerned about creating a
society that not only brings about equality for women, but also an improved world for women and men living together. While this thought-
provoking conversation among feminists keeps evolving, many married
couples are wrestling with very basic issues that (to them) are burn-

ing and no less current. The reality is that they are trying to catch up with 1963, while theorists are carving their way into the 21st century. Raw problems still foment when once-dutiful wives want paying jobs while their husbands find identity in being the chief breadwinner. In such cases, wives can be championed by workshops, informal classes, and shelves of self-help books. But even though men have run the world, individual husbands did not have similar support systems when the revolution of 1963 hit their doorstep.

Men who got married in a more traditional past are often coping for the first time with the results of rigid gender role behavior, and are suffering bitterly. On the other hand, husbands who were at the vanguard of the Civil Rights Movement and Women's Liberation also despair due to the strain of putting theory into practice.

Betty Friedan Revisited

Leo Stojovic and David Meade married their wives in the sixties. A year before their wedding, David gave Jacqueline Meyers a hardback edition of *The Feminine Mystique*. In 1988, Leo sneaked a peek at a copy in the public library. David calls himself a feminist, but Leo also did as much as he could to support his wife's new goals.

For most of his married life, Leo, age 54, marked clear boundaries between the duties of husbands and wives. But desperate to save his marriage, he eventually assumed the lion's share of domestic responsibilities while employed as a civil engineer for a steel manufacturing company. "I was the guy who took care of the kids. I wrote the notes to school. While my wife was doing her thing, a middle-class lady working and catching up on what she missed by becoming a mom—I was *the man*!"

Leo Stojovic lived in his parents' home in a small town in western Pennsylvania, contributing to the family income until he was 27. Then he married Cathleen Shields, six years his junior, who had left home for good at 18 to work as a secretary for a national airline.

Eyes brimming with tears, Leo remembered his wedding day in the summer of 1964. "Our wedding was right out of *The Deerhunter,* a real authentic ethnic Russian celebration. Everybody yelled, 'Horka, Horka,' and I kissed the bride. Our gifts were mostly cash, and a slipper of money was collected for our future children. But 20 years later, out of the blue, Cathleen said she did not love or respect me. She wanted to be a career woman. She brought up things I never thought about, including the fact that I had insisted on a big wedding, which she didn't want. Christ, I thought she enjoyed it."

The Stojovics spent a six-month honeymoon in Europe, courtesy of Cathleen's reduced airfare privileges. A year later, when Leo's company offered him a chance to work on a project in Germany, Cathleen eagerly joined him. Their two children were born in Munich.

Leo accepted more opportunities to work abroad, even living in the Soviet Union for a few months. Leo explained that he loved his wife and did not want to be retired before they were able to see the world together. Wistfully, he commented, "Perhaps I achieved that and lost something else. I wanted a partner with mutual interests, and to share a family. When we married, I had no reason to suspect that I would have less than that." Leo stopped to add, "My life was never guided by material things. I think Cathleen would have liked a bigger house and a Cadillac, but that never meant much to me."

Their marriage was placid until 1980 when the children were teenagers, and Cathleen wanted to return to work. Stunned by this development, Leo says that while he did not appreciate "what the hell was happening to women sociologically, I didn't offer any real objections to Cathleen. Pretty soon she was working full-time as a legal secretary, and the meals weren't so great. I really didn't understand what was happening, but I didn't look around me either."

Leo described how his home life grew worse. "After a year or so, Cathleen said she didn't love me, had no respect for me. Christ, that really hit me hard. I cried. I couldn't understand her reasoning. I can't say I was the best individual in the world. I liked a few drinks. But I was a good provider, a pretty good guy. I always paid all the bills, did what I had to do. Immediately, I went to the yellow pages to find psychiatric help. I just went down the alphabet. But Christ, it's as hard to get an appointment with a psychiatrist as it is with a lawyer. Finally, I just said, 'Take it easy,' and moved out for six months, the worst period of my life. I stayed at the Y for a while and then got an apartment close to the house. I was always stopping by to check the refrigerator, to see the kids."

During their separation, Leo tried to be honest with himself. For the first time, he kept a diary, which helped him to admit his short-comings, such as not being helpful around the house. Then, like a cloistered nun confessing that she had paid off the grocery boy to smuggle in issues of *Playgirl*, Leo sheepishly divulged, "I even went so far as to go to the library to find Betty Friedan's book to see what the hell was in it. I didn't think much of it. But then again, maybe I do have to side with her. A woman's role isn't just to clean the house."

Leo interrupted his story to philosophize, "I never said that my wife had to do all the cleaning and washing and cooking for me. Women's lib just went too fast. People got on the bandwagon too fast. It's all very difficult. Who the hell has the answer? I don't. I want to write a book about my own marriage and call it *Shell-Shocked* or maybe *Time Bomb*."

One evening after dinner with Cathleen in a French restaurant and, Leo searched for a euphemism, "a very satisfying relationship back at my apartment," he returned home. Cathleen continued working as a legal secretary and earned a certificate to be a paralegal. Leo assumed the role of chief caretaker of their two teenage children.

But within a short time, Leo felt that Cathleen was misinterpreting what it meant to be an emancipated woman. Rarely was she home with the family for dinner. Up until then, Cathleen had been a loving mother. Now, she was seldom on the scene. Leo concluded that Cathleen was trying to catch up with what she had missed by starting a family at a young age. "She got interested in jazz, started aerobics, played on a baseball team, took tap-dancing lessons. It was something else!"

Describing himself as a "pseudo-single parent," Leo never confronted Cathleen about how her behavior troubled and inconvenienced him. "I was super-passive, henpecked because I desperately wanted to maintain the integrity of the family. I kept trying to work things out through evasion." After four years, Leo grew weary. "I thought, Hell, this isn't getting better. We weren't at each other's throats, but our life was very poor, and I couldn't take anymore."

The real turning point for Leo occurred in December 1987, when he withdrew $3,000 from their joint savings account to surprise Cathleen with a mink coat. But a few days before Christmas, Cathleen announced that she was moving out, and was aware that he had taken the money from the bank. To retaliate, she cleaned out the remaining $6,000 and left Leo with less than five hundred. Chagrined to learn that Leo had spent the money on a fur coat, Cathleen listened to the options he offered: return the mink, or come up with the payment toward their son's second semester tuition. Cathleen kept the coat, and paid the $2,500 deposit.

The Stojovics' lifestyle never benefited from Cathleen's annual income of $12,000. Leo claimed that she spent it on clothes and dinners with her divorced friends. "But I guess it's hard for a lady to keep up her appearance to compete with younger girls in the office," Leo speculated. "When Cathleen left, she told me that she would rather have been single, a career woman without children. She was seeing a woman psychologist who told her to do what she wanted to do. Shit or get off the pot. I guess that gave her confidence to make her decision!"

During their first separation in 1984, Leo saw a psychologist for only a few sessions. Essentially, he depended upon himself and his diary. "But by 1990," he added, "I knew I had given it my best shot. I also knew I was part of the failure. The marriage didn't work, so what the hell are you going to do?"

With an ironic laugh, Leo described himself as a "liberated man. I'm free now to do what I want, when I want to do it. But I know that single life isn't really for me. I'd like to marry again, but not a divorced woman. I don't want to deal with all those problems. I'd rather marry a widow. Death is a more natural loss. Sharing and communicating are important to me. If you can't share in life, it's very lonely. I talk to the cats."

Husbands such as Leo Stojovic are not downright opposed to their wives' achieving economic independence. In fact, Leo gave Cathleen $10,000 to start a paralegal program and accrue some college credits. Believing that he did everything possible to support her financially, Leo did not feel guilty about Cathleen's leaving. But loneliness and embarrassment did plague him because "divorce is sad and very personal. The worst part was having to talk about my problems to a goddamn lawyer."

Honest about his bewilderment, Leo could not conceptualize a

different reality of marriage, even though he lived out behavior traditionally expected of a wife. He has shifted, nevertheless, from accepting rigid role definitions to expressing ambivalent questions about their
implications. His married life verifies the cyclical rhythm of the
women's movement. While feminist theory keeps evolving toward the
design of a future society, couples earnestly cope with issues that were
novel in the sixties.

One cannot imagine Leo Stojovic, for example, ever reading *The
Feminine Mystique* in 1963, but he did thumb through it more than
20 years later. Ruefully, he tried to understand how his *Deerhunter*
marriage ended in a divorce court. When wives experiment with the
expression of their newly discovered needs, husbands accustomed to
"bringing home the bacon" flounder in their efforts to adapt their own
behavior. Leo and Cathleen Stojovic lacked a mutual vocabulary for
untangling their problems. By contrast, American Feminism grapples
with blueprints that create new strategies for life in the century ahead.

Faded Promises of the Sixties

Quite different from the Stojovics, David and Jacqueline Meade
were among the first young advocates of Women's Liberation. But
shared ideology does not guarantee that a couple will be able to resolve
the intersecting tensions of career and family. Credos are tested by
the intrusion of real life.

In college and graduate school during the sixties, David and Jacqueline were Civil Rights supporters, anti-war demonstrators, and
advocates of the second wave of Feminism. They assumed that Jacqueline would never imitate the traditional role of their mothers. "Yet,"
David pondered, "we never thought through the consequences of these
changes on us. We just assumed that we would have careers, a house
and children, and that everything would be fine. We never thought
about children being a problem until it became one."

David and Jacqueline finished each other's sentences from the age
of 14 on. Teenage sweethearts from a Connecticut town, they were
accepted at Cornell and began living together during their sophomore
year. Such rebelliousness displeased Jacqueline's parents, but not so
much as her decision to marry David in her junior year. When they

cut off Jacqueline's tuition, David was not able to support her and also keep his scholarship aid. That she could not begin her bachelor's degree until after David graduated and then finished architecture school was traumatic for both of them. The Vietnam War further delayed their lives because David was drafted as a graduate student. Bored with clerical jobs for these five years, Jacqueline waited for the day when she could complete her undergraduate requirements and begin her doctorate.

David shared this goal with Jacqueline, shaking his head at the unfairness. "It was terrible that she had to wait so long. We had identical lives, the same intelligence and backgrounds. I wanted every opportunity for her that I had. But we were not prepared to deal with the consequences of juggling my career, Jacqueline's career, and then the additional burden of children. We had never thought it all through in terms of the reality of the demands that we would have to face to make it all work out."

Strains first appeared when David and Jacqueline entered separate spheres—he as an architect with a Manhattan firm, and she as a graduate student in film at Columbia University. They invested so much energy into being successful in their new worlds that they grew farther apart as a couple. Yet, they never revealed their unhappiness to each other.

David explained, "We had known each other so long and so intimately that even when we were in our early twenties, we acted like a long-married couple. We spoke a shorthand. We simply did not talk about every issue that bothered us. We were trapped in adolescent behavior patterns. No matter how unhappy we were, we acted according to long-established habits of relating or not relating that we relied on from the time we were 14 years old."

David and Jacqueline maintained the status quo in their marriage until their second child was born. Caring for an infant was not an impossible task when Jacqueline was writing her doctoral dissertation. Child care became the central issue of the couple's life, however, when Jacqueline accepted a tenure-track position in a New Jersey college.

David remembered, "We simply were not prepared to cope with the burden of children. We were constantly angry, in bad moods, and emotionally drained. In the early days of Women's Liberation, the thrust of the message was to get women out of the home and away from traditional roles. We just never thought about how children would be integrated into all of this. It was silly for us to think that Jacqueline's role could change so dramatically from our mothers', but that my role would stay the same as our fathers', and that things could continue to work well. It's like redesigning one wing of an airplane. It's not going to fly better. It's going to crash. You either have to redesign both wings at the same time, or leave it alone. But we were very idealistic and thought we could be very modern. But it all caught up with us."

The Meades had babysitters and housekeepers and used child-care facilities, but none of these arrangements pleased David, who resented the fact that other women were influencing his children at impressionable ages. He described Jacqueline as "suffering mother's guilt, but she knew that this had to be done or she couldn't continue her career." Time became the overriding reality in David's life. "Professional demands made Jacqueline measure out the time she spent with the children, and then with me. She wasn't supportive of me, and I was not an emotional crutch for her." David and Jacqueline separated and had the best psychologists and psychiatrists for therapy and counseling for two years, together and alone.

David never dreamed that they would not reunite until therapy forced him and Jacqueline to talk about their problems with each other. "Quite simply, we realized that what each needed from the other, the other was not in a position to give. Jacqueline was unable to devote time to the children the way I wanted my wife to do, nor be supportive of me in the way I needed. And I knew that I was precisely the same way with her. I didn't help with the kids as much as she needed, and I was in no position to help her balance her life. We were still in love with each other, but we couldn't work things out. I was miserable in the relationship."

For the first time, David also learned about Jacqueline's fleeting affairs with two academic colleagues. Intellectually, he accepted her cheating as a symptom of how alienated he and Jacqueline had become. Nonetheless, he was furious at her disloyalty and forced the issue of divorce when he also felt justified in having extramarital relationships. By this time, David says they were happy to end their marriage without "murdering each other."

The situation of the Meades is a variant on the more typical problem where a couple, like the Stojovics, cannot adjust to the freedom of changing roles. The simple justice of the argument of *The Feminine Mystique* was so compelling to both David and Jacqueline that they did not think beyond it. But in retrospect, David labeled the first wave of post-Friedan couples as the "lost generation," doomed to be failures because they had no role models, and "society was enormously unhelpful."

David has lived with the real challenges faced by a career couple committed to feminist theory of the sixties. He also knows that his story may not elicit sympathy. Nevertheless, he contributed to an understanding of failed marriages from the honest perspective of a husband who wanted a chance to have it all, a successful career-wife and a happy family. He described the collapse of his marriage as "devastating. I had invested all of my teen years and adult life in one person. The loneliness was terrible. Besides that, we were both always successful in our careers, and not used to experiencing failure."

David remained conversant and analytical about the goals of feminism, believing that values of nurturance should be at the heart of all our institutions so that parental leaves and flex time, for example, are available to both husbands and wives. "There's no reason," he continued, "that the important roles women played in previous generations have to be carried out exclusively by women. If society had more respect for child care and keeping a home, more men would share in it. This is the direction that society is taking, but it's too late for me and my generation. Just as Women's Liberation was too late for our mothers. Something has to be done about men's roles; we have to redesign both wings of the airplane." But David was not about to tinker.

Half of David's week was devoted to shared custody for his young sons. Yet he says that if a "woman is going to have children with me, she has to assume most of the burden. I can't change the demands of my professional life." David knew divorced women with young children who would be willing to accept these terms for marriage. "But women who have been housewives all of their lives bore the shit out of me."

David Meade never believed that a wife should subordinate herself to the needs and desires of a husband and children. After all, as a sympathetic advocate of feminist theory in the sixties, he gave his future wife a copy of *The Feminine Mystique*. Yet powerful traditional attitudes surfaced in him when he was actually called upon to test gender roles in his own marriage. David believed that parenting should be a shared responsibility, allowing women to be as independent as men, and men to be as nurturing as women. But he allowed the risk of reinventing motherhood to the next generation, not his.

David Meade truly believed in the women's movement. As college students, he and his wife imagined themselves in the future living out the values of a new social structure. When we try to understand why such a goal becomes personally unattainable, we give more attention to the experiences of women. But the stories of men are relevant if the quandaries posed by a dual-career marriage are not to be seen as single-sex issues. Obstacles to divorce will be generated when men join women in providing insight into why their difficulties became irreconcilable. By silencing men, or not listening carefully to what they say, other "lost generations" of couples will lose the opportunity to test their ideals of marriage against the realities that ex-husbands and ex-wives face together each morning.

Far less truth is available during the discussion of divorce when the voices of men are suppressed or filtered through the interpretive words of those who trust only the perspective of women. In dismissing a masculine point of view, we obliterate opportunities for arriving at creative solutions regarding the future state of married life. Understanding the difficulties that men experience in marriage is a positive step toward erasing the boundaries of gender differences that stifle men and women, keeping them from solving problems together. Without knowing how men explain their failed marriages, we are guilty of redesigning only one wing of the airplane, a guarantee for a tragic course of events.

DIVORCED FATHERS AND
SEXUAL POLITICS

*Yet it was the thought of telling Judith—the im-
age of her, their first baby, walking between them
arm in arm to the bridge—that broke him. The
partition between himself and the tears broke.*

from "Separating," by John Updike

IN CONVENTIONAL WISDOM, sexual politics in marriage refers to the
control that husbands exert over their wives. The drama of divorce
is then reduced to a predictable conflict between male power and female passivity. A current mode within feminism wants to draw the
curtain on this old plot by concentrating on the power of women, em-
phasizing their choices, rather than dwelling on their victimization.
It is ironic, however, that husbands also have their reasons for feeling powerless but are seldom invited to express as much.

In a child's development, for example, fathers are identified with
competition, ambition, and aggression; mothers with compassion,
caring, and nurturing. But to assume that women are always more caring and nurturing parents than men minimizes the complex range of
female behavior. This presumption also reinforces the false belief that
the only model for fatherhood is the detached and preoccupied dad.
The frustrations, limitations, and joys of single parenting are also experienced by men. The single father simply does not have the information and encouragement that is available to single mothers.

We are not completely at home with images of the sensitive father,
unless he masquerades as "Mrs. Doubtfire." We allow few opportu-

nities to hear the various voices of fathers who adapt their personal lives and alter their work schedules to maintain a loving home. To hear their stories rewrites the definition of sexual politics.

Fathers Are Forever

Bernie Norton first spotted Kay Eliott, a "platinum blonde with a Colgate smile," in a dance contest during happy hour in a bar in Vail, Colorado. He elbowed his way through the crowd, determined to meet her. Their first date ended after dinner and a goodnight kiss because Kay had another date later in the evening.

Keeping his promise, Bernie arrived at her chalet at noon the next day with skis on his shoulder, but planted them in the snow for 24 hours when Kay answered the door wearing a nightgown. For the duration of his holiday, even teasing from his Cleveland friends could not lure Bernie away from Kay. After ten days, they left Vail together and spent two weeks at her home in St. Paul, Minnesota. While there, Bernie did not meet Kay's two preschool daughters because they were visiting with her parents in Michigan.

Bernie could easily take time away from work because he was a pharmacist for his family's chain of drugstores. For the next two months, he took advantage of his position by flying every weekend between Cleveland and St. Paul. Explaining why, Bernie said, "I was magnetized to Kay by an elemental power, a sexual force, and because we had the very same taste in just about everything." He could hardly wait to introduce Kay to his family at his brother's wedding in Oradell, New Jersey. But driving the Pennsylvania Turnpike, Bernie suddenly grew embarrassed just thinking about her meeting his uncle, a Roman Catholic priest. So, at the Valley Forge exit, he suggested that they get married. And they did.

Kay left her position as a commercial interior designer in the Twin Cities. Bernie marveled, "She picked up and moved to Cleveland. And I was an instant father, all within three months." Bernie enjoyed entertaining his many friends in their new condominium, furnished with objêts d'art and Oriental rugs that Kay shifted back and forth from the antiques store that she bought. Business was so successful that she opened another. Within a year, Kay and Bernie moved into a five-bedroom home with a swimming pool in Shaker Heights, Ohio, and bought a ski chalet in the Alleghenies.

However, Kay's new home satisfied her for only a few months. When a bigger house, four doors away, went on the market, she wanted it. Bernie knew they could not afford to move, but, he admitted, "I could never say no because I feared losing her. I gave 200 percent in the marriage, but my money and emotions were being pushed to the limit. Besides buying the house, we joined two country clubs and always had new cars." To increase his capital, Bernie left the family chain of drugstores and diversified his business interests in hazardous waste disposal and trucking.

But financial pressures did not cramp Bernie's exuberance at the birth of his daughter. "I wanted to be as involved as possible with her from the very beginning because I had experienced little warmth from my own parents. I never heard them say 'I love you' to each other, or to their children. I wanted to be absolutely opposite from them as a parent. I was in the delivery room when Tracy was born. The doctor let me cut the umbilical cord. It was the greatest moment of my life." This truly was the moment of Bernie's bonding with Tracy. She was two years old when Bernie and Kay separated, but Tracy lived with Bernie until she was eight.

When Tracy was an infant, Kay ran the two antique shops, while Bernie continued his rigorous work schedule. But he also spent most evenings babysitting the three young children. Kay blamed her absences from home on customers who could see her only in the evening. In truth, her gynecologist and minister were among those who detained her, enchanted less by the mystery of old tapestries than the spell of her sexual vigor. Yet, Bernie believed Kay's excuses. "I loved her so much, I was gullible. Then I began to think that her erratic behavior was caused by a hormonal problem, so I made an appointment to see her gynecologist. I learned later that they were in the middle of an affair."

Bernie was dumbfounded to hear that Kay was scheduled for outpatient surgery the very next morning, but the doctor would not tell him why. Kay denied to Bernie that she was about to be hospitalized.

She insisted that she was packing to attend an antiques fair in Williamsburg.

Convinced that Kay was having an abortion, Bernie greeted her when she was wheeled back from the recovery room. "You have to understand," he emotionally explained, "that I didn't care if she was having an abortion. I wanted this woman. I loved her. I didn't want my daughter raised in a broken family. But when Kay saw me, she screamed, 'I hate your fucking guts.' Then I started to cry. I thought we had a perfect relationship. I was uncontrollable. I went to the cafeteria and was shaking and sobbing. Someone asked me if it was a boy or a girl. The doctor was there and only then told me that Kay had had a tubal ligation. That was unnerving because I had a vasectomy after Tracy was born. I realized that Kay just wanted a license to play around."

Bernie left home, but managed to tap into the telephone lines. Listening to her conversations, he learned that Kay was simultaneously having flings with her gynecologist, the minister, and a neighbor. Regardless, he frequently spent the night, or grabbed, at her convenience, two or three hours in bed. He explained, "No matter what else was going on between us, or maybe because of what was going on, we had great sex. But it was bribery. She would say, 'I'll go to bed if I can have that rug or that piece of furniture.' I'd give her anything, just to have sex for only an hour. I kept thinking that if she could give me love for a little while, then she might even return."

Bernie's physical health declined. He went from 175 pounds to 150. "A medical doctor told me that I was on my way to a complete breakdown. I cried all the time. I couldn't eat. I saw a therapist, but nothing was making sense. A neighbor finally asked, 'Have you tried praying?' She fried me an egg sandwich. I thought it was the best thing I had ever eaten. I began to pray. I didn't know what to say, but I regained some strength by praying and reading the Bible." In the meantime, Bernie still visited Kay for sex. He left home permanently when she asked that he stay away during the week and drop by only on weekends.

Humiliated by this request, Bernie willingly gave Kay the houses and cars, if he could just escape from her and have his daughter. Kay wiped out their savings and checking accounts. Bernie's retirement plan was long depleted because he had borrowed against it to finance their new businesses. Bernie said with sadness, "I had never seen a mother sell a child. But that's essentially what happened." Bernie was granted custody of Tracy, and in the next two years, Kay only visited her twice.

Financially impoverished, Bernie moved with his baby daughter from Ohio to West Virginia to start a new life. He could not return to the family's drugstores because his brothers were angry that he had left them for so many other ventures. He took a job as a salesman for a pharmaceutical company because he could arrange flexible hours for taking care of Tracy. The father and daughter were a happy family, living in a little house and managing on an annual salary of $18,000. When Kay, who had moved to Florida, petitioned for custody after Tracy's sixth birthday, the court denied her request. By this time, Bernie missed Cleveland and felt that Tracy should have the benefit of family ties. Making amends, Bernie returned to the family drug stores, and Tracy's world expanded to include grandparents, cousins, aunts, and uncles.

But at age eight, after returning from a visit with Kay and her two stepsisters in Orlando, Tracy pensively told Bernie, "I love you *and* Mom." No longer the innocent baby, she knew that her parents were locked in a new custody battle. It pained Bernie to watch Tracy's grades fall and see her develop nervous tics. He made the wrenching decision to give her up. "Tracy was carrying an incredible emotional load. I finally realized that either Kay or I had to give. We couldn't cut Tracy in half. I had given everything I had to Kay— houses, equity, antiques—so that I could keep my daughter. And then I gave her my daughter, too. Now Tracy was old enough. Kay wouldn't have to change diapers."

After she left, Bernie could not open the door to Tracy's bedroom for six months. "Anything to do with children could make me cry," he said quietly. "Even kids on TV commercials."

Bernie knew he needed therapy. He began private sessions with a clinical psychologist twice a week. He also found solace in a renewal of his religious faith. "I talked to a priest face-to-face and found myself confessing. He was human, understanding, forgiving. I felt tremendous relief telling him about my past. He didn't moralize. I didn't need that. I still see him about once a month."

Bernie also values the friendships he developed with women. "They have helped me through a lot of heartache. I think women who have been used themselves can be very sympathetic to divorced men. But I'm not about to venture into another marriage. I want someone to laugh and cry with, be comfortable with for a good many years, but I'm gun-shy. I'm always ready for a woman to say 'It's over.' I'm still dealing with echoes."

Even though he still copes with unresolved problems, Bernie no longer feels like a helpless sufferer. His most effective therapy, he claims, has been to leave his problems aside in order to help others experiencing hard times. For example, he informally counsels men going through divorce. He has organized support services for AIDS patients, especially for afflicted children and their parents. He also provides medicine for homeless shelters. He is known in his community as a real friend to people in crisis.

Bernie Norton's primary goal for the first eight years of his daughter's life was to be a good father. Even though Tracy now lives with her mother, Bernie's intentions have not changed. In fact, during a follow-up conversation a few months after our interview, Bernie was touched that Tracy had telephoned to tell him that she had had her first period.

As a transition into the 21st century, the discussion on gender issues could benefit by including men like Bernie Norton who live out versions of female experience. Voices like his soothe the rift between the sexes because he is not ideological. Rather, he spoke about personal problems that are thought to be more typical of women: sexual exploitation, sexual harassment, and the restrictions of gender role behavior.

During our interview, Bernie often struggled through tears trying to express how he felt when betrayed by his wife, what it meant for him to take care of his daughter, and how he grieved when she left to live with her mother. Furthermore, he tried to heal himself by compassionately responding to the suffering of others. The action he is taking now is compatible with Carol Gilligan's analysis in *A Differ-*

ent Voice: Psychological Theory and Women's Development, which states that caretaking and nurturing are central to women's ethical sensitivities and moral code of behavior. Commentaries like Bernie Norton's contribute to our larger understanding of the common ground that men and women share. If the conversation could move beyond blame, gender warfare need not be inevitable.

A Second-Shift Father

In contrast to Bernie Norton, whose faith in himself was renewed through therapy, prayer, and service to others, Ed Switzer depended only on himself and was a prisoner of his hostility toward his wife. He wanted to leave no doubt about the stress he felt as a single parent trying to balance work with providing a home for his two teenage daughters.

In her groundbreaking book, *The Second Shift: Working Parents and the Revolution at Home*, Arlie Hochschild proposes that with two-career parents, the domestic workload dramatically tips toward the wife's disadvantage. But before such timesheets became public, Ed Switzer never considered that he was putting in overtime as a house-husband. Yet, every day, the household shift was his.

His wife Helen did not hold a job. She was not involved in community service. Neither did she enjoy working in their home. In the mid-seventies when their children were school age, Helen wanted freedom from the responsibilities of family, but did not seek a divorce. Instead, she left Indianapolis for New York City, originally her home, to enroll in photography courses, she said, at the Lincoln Center extension of Fordham University. Facetiously, Ed interjected, "Courses like that were just not possible in Indianapolis. You have to understand that as a New Yorker, my wife thought that anything west of the Hudson was frontier. I tolerated her moving because I was in love with her; I acted like a fool, hoping she'd get over this crazy nonsense. It was a while before I could face that she wanted out."

A year before Helen's departure, Ed, a systems engineer, left a secure position in corporate sales to start his own small manufacturing company. Recognizing Helen's unhappiness at home, he wanted her to work in his office so that they could develop common goals.

But after two months, Helen quit. When the business failed to make a profit at the end of the first year, her interest diminished even more.

"The closest she ever came to understanding my work," Ed grimaced, "was to meet me at the office on the way to lunch. She was always cold and distant when I returned from business trips. We lacked intimacy, but I consoled myself by thinking that that's what happened in a marriage. That it lost its fun and became a responsibility. I have always believed in marriage as a contract, that you do what you have to do, especially when you have kids. I was raised a Catholic, but I never thought I'd go to hell if I were divorced. It just took a long time for me to realize that divorce could happen to me. Some people enter marriage thinking that divorce is always possible. But I'd just as soon never be divorced. I believe in commitment."

Ed marked a visit to a marriage counselor as the beginning of Helen's journey out. Ed's perception was that the counselor simply told Helen "to do whatever you want to do to make yourself happy." Helen was always self-indulgent, and the counselor encouraged her to do her own thing. Helen had the excuse she needed, and left for New York. "Beware low-cost counseling," Ed advised.

For three years, Ed paid for Helen's living expenses and the rent for her Greenwich Village apartment. He maintained the home in Indianapolis for their two daughters, and maintained the ruse that their mother was pursuing serious academic goals in Manhattan. In truth, he knew that she had dropped the only course that she had begun, and was sleeping with a series of younger men.

"I was a fool. I was humiliated." Ed tensed. "Helen would tell me about her affairs. She was 40 years old and dating men 20 years younger. She took great delight in fooling them about her age. She even altered the birth date on her driver's license. But I was in love with her, and I thought she would get this out of her system."

While Ed was on a two-week vacation with his daughters, Helen cleared out the Indianapolis home. She did not ask for custody of the children. But while Ed had kept her reputation immaculate with the girls, Helen told them that she had been forced to leave their father three years earlier because of his cruelty.

From 1981 to 1988 when Ed was a single parent, his small manufacturing company struggled for survival because of the floundering steel economy. Often he would drive 200 miles round-trip to see a client in order to be with his children in the evening. "I tried to avoid finding sitters to stay overnight because I learned that the TV sit-com types just do not exist. When the girls had strep throats, broken ankles, and mono, I was there taking care of them, arranging for help, buying groceries, going to school plays, and trying to keep my business going. Helen did not even attend our older daughter's high school graduation. Yet she still tried to paint a cruel picture of me because it's the only way she can justify why she left them for so many years."

Divorced for ten years, Ed remains bitter. The divorce is still the focus of his life, but not because he stays in love with Helen. "I finally gave up the crazy nonsense that we could get back together, but I'm unhappy because of the legal system. I'm not a victim in the sense that I was forced into poverty, but I am the victim of a system that kept me broke for ten years. I'm a successful businessman, yet I live with the threat of someone taking my money away from me. What should have been a simple divorce turned into a seven-year trial with exorbitant legal fees over the interpretation of a property settlement agreement."

Ed revved up. "Divorce is more complex for a small businessman as compared to a husband with a W-2 income, because we are considered to be crooks, hiding money in Swiss bank accounts. Right from the beginning, I was made crazy by a hearing officer telling me what my business was worth, when I damn well knew its worth wasn't near what he was saying."

After a year of litigation, Helen filed for support, but was denied. Ed felt assaulted by attorneys and accountants, whom he interpreted as saying, "We're coming after you. We'll send in public accountants, and you'll pay for it. We'll value your company at a few million dollars, and Helen will get half of it." Ed laughed. "Of course, none of this was really true. My company was not worth a whole lot. I was on the verge of bankruptcy, but I stopped the divorce proceedings in the face of these accusations, and waited three years for a no-fault divorce."

The property settlement remains a thorny issue for Ed. The court awarded Helen the Indianapolis house, where Ed had been living with their daughters. But when Helen wanted cash, Ed bought the house back from her. "I had to buy my own house twice." He hit the table. What chafed Ed most, however, is the clause, to which he admittedly agreed, stating that he must pay uninsured medical expenses for the children, now 19 and 21.

His older daughter Heather developed chronic headaches after falling from a bicycle during her sophomore year in college. Since then, psychologists, psychiatrists, and neurosurgeons have treated her. A dentist operated for TMJ, but, Ed said miserably, "He messed up her mouth so bad that she had to have orthodontic work. Now I'm paying orthodontists' bills for a second time. And she sees psychiatrists routinely."

Ed knows that Heather was "hurt badly by her mother's absence. She was a withdrawn, insecure child, but we never could talk about what Helen had done. She would hear us arguing, I'm sure, about Helen's affairs. When we were in the process of divorcing, we saw a psychologist who predicted that Heather would have emotional scars."

When Ed told Helen that a high-priced psychiatrist did not seem to be effective in helping Heather, Helen filed contempt-of-court charges for his failure to pay the psychiatrist's fees. Helen lost. Ed explained that he did not shirk from assuming his daughter's tuition or health care expenses. He simply wanted to work out with Helen a plan of medical care for Heather, since he was bearing the expenses. But Helen's attorney would not move on this issue until Ed paid the legal fees generated by Helen for the contempt charge.

Currently, Ed is frustrated, cranky, and bitter. Helen remains his nemesis. "I've been over her for years," he said wearily, "but I can't move forward because of how she tries to alienate my daughters. She tells them that I pay their bills only because of the agreement we have, that I really do not care about them. I've been accused of caring only about money. But the money has to come from somewhere. Our divorce was about money from the beginning. Never about child custody. Helen walked out on them and stayed away. Now she's trying to destroy my credibility with my kids, and it's got me awfully mad.

"Now that they are older and can see more, she has no way to justify having left them except to make it sound like my fault. Last year, I made $85,000, more than I have ever made in my life. But after taxes and paying all the kids' tuition and bills, I'm broke. I'd be paying tuition and medical bills if we were still married, but I'm bitter that I'm so hassled by Helen and the courts. It makes you nuts to be involved in the same legal matters for so long. I don't feel that the legal system does justice to a man when these things happen."

Ed encourages his daughters to spend time with Helen, even though he is troubled by what she says about him. "All daughters need to have a mother. Helen is very generous with them now. She's married a multimillionaire and lives in an apartment overlooking Central Park. It's easy to be a rich guardian angel indulging children on shopping sprees and European vacations. But she wasn't there for their sore throats and skiing accidents. I was the one who put in the time. She was nowhere in sight. Heather has emotional problems, but now she's seduced by her mother's wealth and gifts, even though she sees a battery of doctors."

Ed thinks about remarrying, but legal problems and his business absorb his attention. Nonetheless, he talked about the qualities he values in a wife, and offered a definition of a sound marriage. He favors self-confident, achieving women because Helen grew resentful for being financially dependent upon him. Warming up to his analysis, Ed concluded that Helen absorbed a value system that advocated the notion that a "good wife" should be in-service to her husband and children. Ed knew that this role would inevitably be frustrating for her and offered ways out by telling her to finish her bachelor's degree, get a job, or work in the business. "But instead of acting positively," Ed complained, "she ran off to New York and had a bunch of affairs. And she's still justifying what she did by lying about me to my kids. The worst thing for any marriage is for one person to be ultimately dependent on the other. You can't depend upon another person to make you completely happy."

Ten years after his divorce, Ed is still irate. He agreed to be interviewed because he hoped that venting would make him feel better. Nevertheless, he hopes that other men will learn by not following his example in allowing a marriage to drag on. "There is a finality that has to be recognized. Now that I look back, we should have been divorced very early in our marriage. I was in love with Helen then, and it would have been hard, but I could have gone on. Instead, she had ten years of fun, while I lived as a single parent. Divorce proceedings took up the ten best years of my life. I waited too long. Circumstances became too complicated. Divorce should never be the center of one's life for so many years. Move on. Get away from it. Don't do what I did."

Despite the strength of Ed's declaration, his behavior was equivocal. His desperation was still alive and reached into this interview to corner a listener, a reader. His scars remained fresh. He wanted other men to know his story and measure their own cases against it. Yet he could not alter his own behavior. His words plunged him deeper into darkness and sorrow, as if letting go of the past would have really been a sign of weakness. As if the journey toward light is only for the faint of heart.

The Joys of Shared Custody

A divorced man who is very different from Ed Switzer is Jeffrey Montgomery, a university physics professor who shook his head and said, "If you want to talk about my divorce, it's cloudy. It's better for me to step out of it and get on with the new stuff. The old stuff about my marriage has faded, naturally and enforceably by me. We went through stormy weather arguing about custody and money. Now I'm trying to focus on new goals of my own, especially in the context of my children. I try to focus on good things, and good things are children."

Jeffrey Montgomery and Sara Stevens, both born in England, married after completing their undergraduate education, and lived in Oxford while Jeffrey finished his doctorate. At the end of a two-year academic appointment in Australia, Jeffrey returned to Oxford for post-doctoral work, and Sara taught grammar school. They came to the United States 12 years ago when Jeffrey received a lucrative offer from a prestigious university to head a new institute. They have been divorced for five years.

"From the beginning," Jeffrey claimed, "I suspected that our marriage wouldn't last for the long haul. On the other hand, I worked at it and wanted it to. We were married very young before I had worked out a lot of my own bullshit. If I had, maybe it could have been easier on her and me."

Just what the bullshit was, Jeffrey would not say. He refused to dwell on the tensions of sexual politics. From his perspective, the present and the future were the important parts of his story. "The bridge from the past to the present to the future is the most important thing. I knew all the time that no matter how emotionally upsetting the divorce process was, it was like sailing through a storm. If I hung on, and held on, with strong faith in myself and my hand on the tiller, I could come out on the other side of it. I could eventually be a much happier and better person, and a model for my sons. I love them, and knew I had a lot to share with them."

Jeffrey eagerly talked about his relationship with his sons. He believes that many men lose patience with divorce proceedings, and move out of state or remarry quickly and emotionally abandon their children. But Jeffrey wanted to be as active as possible in his children's lives by having shared custody. "There are bad feelings going through divorce because it's all about money and time. Men want to pay off and give up. I knew it would not ultimately be fulfilling to me in the long term and a disaster to the lives of my children if I said 'the hell with this. I'm going to leave it all.' Even when my sons are in their twenties and thirties, I think the influence of fatherhood is important. Now I realize in my forties what strong emotional ties I have with my father. I want to have an enduring relationship with my sons as well.

"I knew I would have a better shot at that by being separated than in a marriage filled with arguments and strife. But neither could I remain close to them by moving to the fringe of their lives now. If I were not so busy," Jeffrey claimed, "I would like to write a book to help other men feel energetic about fatherhood."

Jeffrey and his ex-wife now reside in different states, New York and Illinois. Their sons live with Sara during the week in Chicago, where Jeffrey also maintains a home so that he can be with them every other weekend, and sometimes more often. He wanted shared custody from the beginning, but agreed with Sara that it would be best for the boys to live with her during the week. Sara and Jeffrey remain polite with each other because Sara values Jeffrey's relationship with their sons, and as parents they want to be able to communicate.

Jeffrey wants to be an "intelligent, joyous father." He left his marriage principally because of the tension that existed between him and Sara. "We tried to work out our problems; the tension was no one's particular fault. But I didn't want to be one of those families where you can feel the strain all around you, coming out of the woodwork and furniture. I didn't want the boys to live in that kind of environment."

On the Sunday afternoon I talked with Jeffrey, his home was filled with the aroma of fresh popcorn and the sounds of an old James Bond film on the VCR. The six-year-old boy greeting me at the door yelled upstairs in a stage whisper, "The lady writer is here, Dad." The household was anything but tense.

While we drank iced tea at a picnic table underneath a scruffy apple tree, Jeffrey pointed out that his 14-year-old son helped him to build the wooden deck. "We have great fun back here," Jeffrey said eagerly. "We grill hamburgers, hot dogs, fish. Sit around and kid each other, tell jokes. This is the world I love about being close to the boys, the real sense of sharing day-to-day experiences and then integrating them towards some whole experience of life. They seem incredibly happy to me. They laugh and enjoy life. They have a robust spirit, which I wanted for them."

Jeffrey's house is filled with the paraphernalia of growing boys: hockey sticks, baseball bats, school bags, a box of Cheerios on the kitchen table. The boys come to this home every other weekend and sometimes for longer stretches. "I don't downplay their mother's home," Jeffrey explained, "but this is home, too. I've made an effort for the kids to have their own rooms and comfortable blankets to lug around. No one wants to feel like a guest in a hotel. Their sports equipment is here. They have to feel as if they're going from home to home."

Jeffrey particularly enjoys being with them on Sunday nights and sending them off to the school bus on Monday mornings. He stressed that he and Sara "are not brittle about keeping rigid schedules with the kids. If I can stay an extra day with them, Sara is very reasonable.

If I pop into town just overnight during the week, I call Sara beforehand to see what plans we can make. I respect her schedule. But we both realize that it's not in our sons' best interest to argue over trifles."

Jeffrey treasures the ordinary times he spends with his children. "It's hard to add up all the small things because each one of them seems so trivial about how great it is to be a father. But the contrived happiness that you see on the Cosby show is a very spontaneous thing right in this backyard. There's a loving mood about the whole thing, whereas before, a family barbecue would have been filled with tension. Now the air is loving and free, without any dramatically high expectations, just the fun of the moment."

Jeffrey also relishes being part of what he calls the "heartbreak times. Each one of the boys has his difficulties, but it's important for me to be a part of those day-to-day struggles like getting a hopeless piece of homework completed. When they're frustrated and tearful, I feel so upset inside. But this is the daily life that I wanted to be a part of. I didn't want to be the knight in shining armor rushing in at holiday times to whisk everybody off to Disney World. And sometimes when I'm getting them off to school, or off to soccer practice, I do act like a major—'eat your Cheerios; get your tie on; get organized for God's sake.' But what's remarkable is that I enjoy all of that small stuff. Yet, all of that small stuff used to piss me off to the max when I was in a marriage that wasn't doing any good for anybody."

When Jeffrey and Sara separated, the boys were seven, four, and one. Jeffrey estimates that 18 months passed before he was out of the storm. He knew, however, that unless he "put in time in literally minuscule acts, by the time the boys were ten, my relationship with them wouldn't add up to anything. I didn't think that I could choose some arbitrary age and then enter magically into their lives to be an active father. I know that trust and love are all about adding up little grains of sand in the balance."

Jeffrey explained that "riding out the storm" meant "getting in touch with my feelings. I may seem very relaxed, almost phlegmatic now, but I had to figure out what was truly important to me. This sounds terribly maudlin, but I had to be honest with myself and get some answers. Then it was easier for me to give and to love others. It works."

Jeffrey offered no prescription for instant success as a divorced father. He wants to create a happy environment for his children because he believes that the effects will be long-lasting in their relationship with him. He celebrates the ordinary. "If it's hard for men to make contact with the day-to-day bullshit stuff," Jeffrey shrugged, "at least through some project fathers and children can be involved. With boys and girls, it can be through sports, skiing for example. I go jogging every day, and my older sons will often run with me. That's a nice feeling—running around the streets with your sons by your side. Repainting the house, I taught them how to use paintbrushes and rollers. The six-year-old paints four feet from the ground."

If fathers feel alienated from their children during divorce proceedings, Jeffrey thinks that "getting back in is easy but requires enormous patience. It requires getting involved in a very relaxed way with all of the tedious stuff in order to develop a level of trust. If they're teenagers, go with them to a rock concert. When you are away, send them a tape or a goofy hat or sweatshirt. All these small things add up. When children know that you are really there for them and want to be a part of their lives, they pick up on that. Not everything is going to work, but I think that's what any friendship is about—even adult relationships—being there for somebody and sharing things with them: walks, meals, telephone calls, ice creams, movies."

Furthermore, if a man can afford it, Jeffrey recommends taking children on a "great holiday two or three times a year because kids want to see their parents having fun. But that's the icing on the cake because vacations in themselves will not work. You have to be there for the small stuff."

What is the state of Jeffrey Montgomery's social life, considering that he spends so much time traveling to spend weekends and vacations with his sons? When asked this question, Jeffrey replied, "What it means is that I don't date at all when I'm really around the children, but not for any other reason except for how busy the weekend is, taking them to soccer games and parties. It's just too hard to juggle children and dates at the same time. On weekends that I don't see them or during the week, I date. When the children are older, I would hope to be closer to somebody and get married again. Right now, it's hard to develop a big romance when I'm so split between two home bases.

But that's fine with me now. That's where I am. In this particular zone of life, I think I'll wait to see what fate delivers."

Since spending so much time devoting himself to his children, Jeffrey thinks that his sensitivity quotient has risen. "My intuitive side has evolved so that I can almost instantly tell if I have the hots for somebody or if they are just dust in the wind." He laughed. "That's been a side bonus of all of this. I have exercised my emotional muscles so much with my children that I really know now who I like and don't, and what will work and won't. And I don't think that I knew that before because my mind had been trained to be a scientist, and all of these other sides of myself had been only somewhat developed through grammar school, but not necessarily to make the best choices. The next time I marry, I'll enter into it with more wisdom. That's a side benefit for men who stay close to their children."

Jeffrey credits his British education for helping him to value the arts. While in grammar school, he read "great literature." He appreciates that he was encouraged to be a musician as well as a scientist. As captain of the rugby team one year, Jeffrey thought about becoming an "outright jock, but the finer side of life was encouraged and appreciated just as much by the British system." Jeffrey still sings, writes music, and plays classical guitar. Occasionally, he gives lunchtime recitals and plays gigs. He enjoys buying CDs his sons like, and then listening with them.

But Jeffrey also remarked, "Things change. Children get older. My 14-year-old is now making his own decisions about where he wants to be. He has spent some long weekends in New York City with me. We went to museums, did some teenage shopping for skateboard clothes, listened to music in the evening. Parents who have shared custody can't be ultimately legalistic. Too much effort is required to stay in that mode, and it inhibits the growth of relationships. If an ex-husband offers a pleasant experience for the child, an ex-wife with a loving heart should realize that. During divorce negotiations, people can seem to be worse than they are. But then there's a time to stop being vindictive. It's better for both parents if they can be reasonable enough with each other to share the decision-making. But when you're going through the stormy times, it's hard to imagine that you'll ever get to that point, or even want to."

Jeffrey Montgomery now concentrates on the future rather than dwelling on the sexual politics of his past. "No amount of rolling around in the muck will get you clean. Acknowledge that you made mistakes and learn from them. Concentrate on making life better the next time around. That's the challenge, and I think it's right."

* * *

Jeffrey Montgomery is an example of a former husband who, after a period of reflective self-consciousness, was able to look at himself, know who he is and what he wants, and take responsibility for making choices that will shape his own development and promote a positive relationship with his family. He concentrates on future possibilities, and offered his story and advice so that other men can transform their lives for the better.

In a different mode, ex-husbands locked in resentment relentlessly focus on the negative aspects of their marriage and divorce. "Concentrate on making life better" are not words in their vocabulary. Their interviews with me provided them an opportunity to vent, a new chance "to roll around in the muck." Describing their marriages, they stressed conflict and avoided any personal crisis. They retold their stories, but their own center remained somewhere in the past. They held the future at bay. Consequently, they never got very far inside their hurt . . . nor very far away.

"WHO AM I NOW? WHAT DID IT MEAN? WHERE AM I GOING?"

GRIEF IN A MAN'S WORLD

The lieutenant, carrying his wounded arm rear-
ward, looked upon them with wonder . . .
Several officers came up to him . . . One, seeing
his arm began to scold . . . His tone allowed one
to think that he was in the habit of being wounded
every day. The lieutenant hung his head, feeling,
in this presence, that he did not know how to be
correctly wounded.

from "An Episode of War," by Stephen Crane

GRIEF IN A MAN'S WORLD is highly suspect. However, when divorced men describe feeling emptiness, loneliness, nothingness, and fear that they are "going crazy," "losing it," or having a "nervous break-down," therapists agree that they are consumed by grief.

When ex-husbands drag through the day, lack concentration, lose or gain weight, suffer insomnia or crave sleep, and feel guilt followed by anger, they are experiencing the normal symptoms of grief. The best prescription is to go through the hurt, and understand why it is there.

Listening to their stories and witnessing their tears convinced me that ex-husbands mourn their marriages more than we currently understand or are prepared to accept. For example, as I talked about my research for *Men on Divorce*, both men and women frequently challenged: "Can you really trust what they are telling you?" Never was I asked that question about women whom I had interviewed for *Divorced Women, New Lives*. But no different from divorced women, ex-husbands also feel excruciating pain.

"Divorce takes an emotional toll on guys, but maybe no one wants to know about that," offered a thirtysomething attorney who practices family law. Yet attorneys are among those who do not want to know. "Perhaps it's because of my practice," one of them speculated, "but it is rare for a man in my office not to be at the point where he cannot accept divorce. A man's reaction largely depends on his economic status. Professionals and business executives are able to see divorce as the dissolution of an economic partnership. They know that provisions have to be made for a wife and children, but they don't feel that the world is coming apart, at least economically. Let's face it: For divorce, it's a man's world. In terms of social and emotional impact, it's not that great."

The stories I have heard from ex-husbands contradict that observation. The lonely withdrawal from married life is very real to them. They express loss in a million different ways. Some men are without solace, barely able to function, and say that "divorce is worse than death." The other extreme is evinced by men who rage rather than mourn. They endure their pain by working longer hours, overindulging in alcohol, or by engaging in frenetic sex or death-defying sporting activities. To show strength, they hide their grief from others, and even from themselves.

Most ex-husbands express their grief somewhere between these polarities. But it is common for all of them, at some point, to feel desolate because loss is an inevitable consequence of divorce.

Anyone who has mourned the death of a spouse may not appreciate the comparison, but death and divorce share similarities. Any experience of loss, regardless of what it is, carries with it similar issues that need to be resolved. In general, the problems of loss include forsaking the camaraderie, companionship, understanding, and compassion of a particular person, and accommodating the loneliness that ensues from separation. Feelings of anger, anguish, confusion, and sadness also need to be worked through. Even men who accept divorce as the best answer for their unhappy marriages confront the ultimate questions that death poses: "Who am I now? What did it all mean? Where am I going?"

According to bereavement experts, when a man's wife dies, the mourning husband will "come to the other side, and ultimately say,

'She is dead and is not coming back.'" But when it comes to divorce, certain aspects of loss become slightly magnified. Cathleen Fanslow-Brunjes, Bereavement Coordinator for Hospice Care of Long Island, New York, made the distinction by saying,

"Bear in mind that with divorce there's not a body to mourn. It's disenfranchised grief. The attendant rituals are missing: there's no wake or funeral. The day the divorce is finalized may pass unnoticed. Family and friends aren't bringing food and casseroles. From society's viewpoint, you couldn't make the marriage work, or you weren't right together anyway. So expressions of grief are somehow unacceptable. Friends grow impatient. If a man has been successful solving problems in his job but can't control his marriage, he's thrown by it. All this works against a man when he feels inside that he has a lot to cry about."

Husbands who are betrayed frequently claim that a wife's death would have been easier to absorb than the reality of her leaving for another man or in search of freedom. Images of death, physical paralysis, and amputation permeate their narratives. There is good reason for this, according to Douglas Gillette, co-author of *King, Warrior, Magician, Lover*. In a telephone interview with me, he commented, "When a man is voted against—when his sexuality, capacity to protect, provide, excite is found wanting—it's a disastrous blow to self-worth. Men feel abandoned. There's no other message when a wife leaves a husband. With death, men can maintain their sentimentality and express grief."

Gillette interprets the feelings of adult male abandonment within the context of Oedipal drama. If the father does not claim his wife from the young boy in a loving way, the son keeps trying to keep mother from father. In his own marriage, he will then translate an unresolved Oedipal attachment into an effort to turn his wife into mother. Rather than have her abandon him or choose another man, he would prefer that she be dead because then "at least he can make her a saint." Nothing is more frightening or damaging to a husband's self-esteem, Gillette told me, than when a wife walks away. Since the end of the marriage feels to him like the loss of mother, he mourns the marriage as if divorce were death.

In addition to exploring the unconscious in order to explain the grief of an abandoned husband, therapists also interpret grief within a situational and cultural context. For example, among husbands immobilized after divorce are those who have been taken care of by their wives almost as if they were little boys. In this childlike position, they turn wives into mothers, and are passive while their "mothers" wait on them. For most couples, this behavior is not the result of a rational decision. But the comfort of being tended to is seductive for men, and wives are slow to see the web they are creating.

Until separation forces them to face how dependent they have been on their wives for daily maintenance, encouragement, and understanding, men generally think they are self-reliant. Regardless of how good or bad the marriage was, many of the ex-husbands I interviewed have described feeling "paralyzed" or "numb," "as if I had a leg cut off," when their wives were no longer available to cater to, and anticipate, their needs. Even in a marriage with sparse communication, a husband's support system is often dismantled when the marriage ends and he is on his own.

Charlie and Elizabeth Butler illustrate the point. Both artists, they considered themselves too aware of social change to keep alive stereotypic gender patterns. But after five years of marriage, Charlie's studio became his mistress. Until the day she left him, Charlie thought Elizabeth was perfectly happy, when indeed she felt as if she were in servitude. "Elizabeth always drove," Charlie points out. "Actually, she had responsibility for *everything* in the house, while her career was second. She was the nurturer and the life-preserver. She was the caretaker, and I was the dependent. I could have gone on forever that way. I was totally comfortable. No wonder I liked being married," Charlie laughed. "I didn't understand what was happening until Elizabeth said making me happy could not continue to be her purpose in life."

When Elizabeth had been gone a week, Charlie felt "incapacitated by a great guilt. For months I was lost and bereft and could not paint. I never felt so immobilized. I did not think I would ever paint again. My parents are still alive, and I've never really experienced death. But I was overwhelmed with grief during my divorce."

Grief Is Inevitable

Grief is not limited, however, to deserted men like Charlie Butler. Their grief may be more intense, but those husbands who are convinced that divorce is in the best interest of themselves and their wives also experience an aching loss. If loss is defined as not being in the same place as before, it is impossible not to have grief when divorce occurs. For many reasons, grief intrudes into the cycle of divorce and bides time. Men who were miserable in their marriages and wanted a divorce are surprised when they feel sad and empty. Yet when couples agree on little else, at one time they did share hope and intimacy. Even when feelings are beyond logic, they are still very real. Without wanting to reverse the decision to divorce, an ex-husband will lament the loss of common bonds and dreams. He may never miss his wife, but may yearn for old relationships with his children, friends, and extended family. He may grieve the loss of home, role, identity, status, and what might have been.

Very often, former husbands are not pining for a lost spouse, but rather the *lost potential* of a perfect marriage. They mourn that they never will have the relationship that they need and want. Even husbands who leave their wives for other women harbor a secret inner space where they mourn the passing of their own lives, a lost time, collected memories that they can never really share.

Grief is a natural, if unexpected, part of the divorce process, but men, in general, are surprised by the force of its demands. Buried deep in our society's subconscious is the stoical image of John Wayne, callous to sadness and heartbreak. While therapists concur that grief is ultimately cured alone, a man moving through divorce often thinks that no one else has ever felt the way he does. At some point in the divorce cycle, a man will feel bereft, helpless, and desolate. But if he silences these feelings, other men have also silenced them. If he feels guilt and embarrassment, so have other men. If he is scared by his confusion, other men have also known that fear.

Grief is not madness, but ex-husbands often endure it as a shameful secret. Grief is so mistaken as a sign of weakness that men will abort their mourning by expressing only anger and hostility, emotions also natural to separation and divorce, but more acceptable for men to vent than sorrow. Finding it easier to verbalize anger than grief, they blame their wives or themselves for causing the marriage to fail.

Dr. Terrance O'Connor, a seasoned therapist from Silver Spring, Maryland, told me that the "major difference in the way men and women experience divorce is that men will not allow themselves to grieve, and women will. But years later, their grief may pour out. The longer a man's grief is pent up, the harder it is for him to let go. If he gets stuck yelling, 'What the hell's wrong with her?', he never grows in self-knowledge, but keeps perpetuating blame. Blame doesn't help the healing process."

Unresolved Grief

Men resist their grief because it makes them feel fragile, unstable, and out of control. They fear that their symptoms are pathological, when, indeed, they are to be expected. If men bury their grief, it will only overwhelm them at another time. I saw this happen during many of my interviews. In the middle of recalling a memory, about one-third of the 45 men I interviewed burst into tears. However, in my discussions with the same number of divorced women for *Divorced Women, New Lives*, no tears were shed.

For example, eight years after his divorce and only months before he was to be remarried, one of my interviewees began to cry as if his divorce had just occurred yesterday. I asked psychologists about this phenomenon, and their explanations were consistent with the interpretation offered by Cathleen Fanslow-Brunjes:

> You allowed the men you interviewed to write their own stories. Men often carry over a macho role into therapy. After a few visits, they solve their superficial problems, feel a little bit better, and never return. They never get to the heart of their grief because they won't stay in therapy long enough. You approached them without an agenda, only to tell their stories. You did not assume the role of a therapist. Grief really doesn't dissipate in time; it accumulates. Consequently, when a man unexpectedly feels [as if

he is] in a safe environment, his grief can gush, even after many years.

Truth resides in personal stories, rather than in abstractions or applied theories, but men have not been adequately united by their stories of divorce to understand the grief they share. In the past 30 years, taboos have relaxed about what is acceptable for a woman to express about her inner life. Not so with men. Role expectations therefore complicate a man's behavioral response to grief in a way not generally experienced by women. Coping with grief is integral to divorce, but compared to the material available on all other aspects of divorce, the subject of men and grief has received little attention. Bereavement experts have, therefore, suggested to me that a divorced man can be reassured that he is not different from other men, and yet is recognizable as himself, if he understands the stages of bereavement. Once he accepts the fact that grief is a normal emotional response to the irretrievable loss of another person, he may gain insight into the range of emotions he is feeling and find solace in knowing that others have been where he is.

Moving Through Grief

The psychological stages that a person goes through while facing the death of a loved one have been adapted by many therapists to illuminate the loss felt by divorced persons. The cycle revealed by Dr. Elisabeth Kübler-Ross in her classic study, *On Death and Dying*, is a pattern of Denial, Anger, Bargaining, Depression, and Acceptance. Variations on these stages are apparent in the personal narratives of men describing their experiences of separation and divorce, but not necessarily according to a predictable formula.

Denial

There are various expressions of denial. A husband and wife may be engaged in divorce talk over months or even years, but all too often a husband has selective hearing and refuses to accept that the conversation is taking place. No matter who initiates the divorce proceedings, his first response may be to repudiate any feelings of loss. To resist dealing with the new circumstances of his life, he may avoid any contact with wife and children, drink heavily, become a workaholic, or have meaningless sex. A man may also avoid self-reflection by filling up his time by overindulging in those activities that he had sporadically engaged in—that is, more golf, more tennis, more sporting events—more of everything. In this stage, a man may also withdraw from family and friends, being unable to speak about his feelings, even to himself. He may feel numb, as if living in a void.

Anger

Anger is felt most intensely by abandoned husbands who feel emasculated or powerless. Embarrassment over their situations may cause them to internalize their anger, rather than display it. Unfortunately, anger turned inward is physically debilitating. For other men, anger is situational. For example, otherwise gentle men may be overtly aggressive, both verbally and physically, with their wives and children. Newly separated men often have sudden outpourings of wrath and hostility, which are shocking even to themselves. In one case that I know of, a previously nonviolent man picked up a tire jack, intending to storm the house of his wife's lover, until he was stopped by his teenage son.

However, men who wish to divorce can also be angry when they find how expensive and lengthy the process can be. They may become infuriated by the new demands and strains on their lives, particularly if these situations involve custody arrangements for children. Men are typically angry when separation and divorce do not grant them the freedom that they expected. They may begin to think: "If only I had done . . . If only she had said," thereby assuming more guilt, pointing more blame, and inflaming their hostility.

Bargaining

Bargaining generally occurs when a marriage is on the rocks, and the husband makes himself vulnerable by promising revolutionary changes that he cannot or will not deliver, such as marriage counseling, sharing housework, more time at home, a better job, more vacations. At this point, the marriage may be beyond repair, and the wife does not want to continue it, even if the promises are fulfilled. The husband will feel even more angry when rejected, and negative emotions will intensify.

Depression

Depression is a normal part of the divorce cycle, but is not to be confused with clinical depression, which occurs when a person is unable to function over a length of time.

Throughout their narratives, the men I interviewed described loss of interest in life, loss of appetite, sleeplessness, and lethargy. They lacked the ability to concentrate, and cognitive skills slipped. Although frightening to experience, these feelings are the rule rather than the exception during the normal stages of grief.

Unfortunately, most men are unprepared for the intensity of these reactions and often fear that they are losing their sanity. Gradually, these emotions diminish, but not according to a rigid standard. Each man must invest in his own recovery. Professional counseling is not necessary if he is willing to understand what is going on in his own life and to discover mechanisms that help him to mourn. The mourning produces its own healing. Nonetheless, waves of pain and loss can be temporarily activated, even to the point of weeping.

Acceptance

The turning point in the grief process begins when the focus of attention gradually shifts from the chaos of the divorce to the reconstruction of a new life. Men know when they have reached this stage, for they dwell less on the past and are more willing to move forward with new challenges and friends. Acceptance does not promise the end of suffering. A song, an image, or a memory may provoke loneliness and wistfulness, because even a marriage ending in divorce probably had its share of happy moments.

As applied to divorce, Kübler-Ross's schemata provides a coherent pattern of recovery. Her linear approach through the stages of loss is helpful to men who wish to understand their feelings within a rational framework. Men accustomed to setting personal, business, and career goals may respond well to a structured strategy, or apply Kübler-Ross's stages in a more rigid way than she ever intended. Other men in the throes of divorce may feel, however, that their conflicting emotions defy categories, analysis, or logic.

While respecting Kübler-Ross's research, psychologists warn that grief cannot be programmed and managed. Rather than imagining the stages of grief as a ladder that one must climb and conquer, they visualize, instead, the steady attention required to peel back layers of grief, like the delicate tissue of an onion, which offers, at last, a center.

Grief Is Tricky

For example, Kimberly Underwood, a therapist from Washington, D.C., specializing in men and divorce, said to me, "It's not up to a therapist to declare, 'You haven't gone through Kübler-Ross's five stages of grieving.' Life is not like that. Grief is tricky. It hides for a while. Some men take two years, others three to six months. The important thing is for a man to have respect for what his feelings are telling him at the time, and follow through with trying to understand why they are there."

Our society has given men little permission to dwell on what they feel and why. We expect them to mask their emotions and focus pragmatically on how to change a situation for the better. By observing Kübler-Ross's stages, a man has a sense of motion, of gaining victory. On the other hand, by observing himself, he marks progress through the pattern of his own individual and unique responses, not by imposed standards that are considered universally normal. Furthermore, he has the opportunity to see the continuity of his life and experience renewal.

Among therapists advocating the advantage of this approach is Dr. A. Barbara Coyne, who was on the nursing faculty at Loyola University and studied with Dr. Kübler-Ross between 1964 and 1967, the time when Kübler-Ross was doing her initial research on death and dying at the University of Chicago hospitals. As a psychotherapist specializing in loss and bereavement, Coyne told me that she no longer applies Kübler-Ross's stages when treating men who are mourning either divorce or death.

Coyne said, "I learned a great deal from her. Her work was a landmark. But like many other therapists, I have put Kübler-Ross into my own frame of reference. Kübler-Ross treats grief in stages, and I don't think it works that way. It's not, 'Well, I've done that piece now and I can move forward.' You don't move along in staged dimensions. I think it's important that a person deals with where he is at this moment rather than where the stages say he should be, where he thinks he should be, or where others tell him he should be. He needs to consider what's happening in his life at the time in order to see his divorce from different perspectives."

Because men generally like to win, they often feel like losers if they zigzag rather than sprint through Kübler-Ross's hurdles. Barbara Coyne continued, "A man will say to me, 'I should be better; it's seven months; I should be at this point, and I'm not.' I try to help him see where he is, what he is feeling, and all of the things that are keeping him stuck there. We always seem to use a dimension of linear time, but awful hurting pain is simply not experienced in linear time. It's not estimable that in months, or days, or weeks a person should be at a certain place. Whatever he is experiencing at the present moment needs to be spoken and respected and received without judgment or labeling."

In place of Kübler-Ross's stages of recovery, Coyne described the process of mourning by using the metaphor of a well-written story that has a beginning, a middle, and an end. A man must have the courage to begin that process, and the courage to end it. Like the well-written story, the beginning moves the reader forward into the middle where the action occurs, and then tapers off and ends. Finishing the narrative does not mean that the reader forgets the story. "It keeps reverberating inside, and we keep thinking about it and learning from it," Coyne maintained. "We may even go back and read a part of it. That's what I mean by not experiencing grief in linear time."

Furthermore, therapists advocating a flexible approach for coping with the loss of divorce indicate that not all men experience each one of Kübler-Ross's stages. They challenge Denial, for example, suggesting that men in the throes of divorce do not deny their situation as much as they find some feelings more difficult to articulate and act upon.

"If a man says, 'I'm mad as hell,' or 'I can't deal with that,' I don't think that's denial," Coyne insisted. "I think people know what's best for them, and when they can approach a topic or back away from it."

Rather than try to meet prescribed stages for recovery, a man may be better helped by observing and owning his feelings. To do this, he has to remove the stereotype that feelings are either bad or a mark of weakness, and accept them as "value free." Feelings then become signposts of growth, indicating where he needs to go next in his life. Instead of saying, for example, "I shouldn't be feeling so angry . . . I shouldn't have said that . . . I shouldn't be crying . . . I should be able to handle this . . . ," a man might permit himself to question why he is feeling angry or sad at that particular time. He might pull toward himself, connecting present and past. Peeling away layers of the onion, he may cry even more. But the process ends in renewal for him. Then, he can come to a deeper understanding of who he is and what he wants his relationship to be with other people.

Applying the vocabulary of literary analysis, Coyne concluded that the process of self-interrogation takes a man inside, to the "inner theater where the drama of his life is really played out. The characters in the drama of our lives are parents, grandparents, spouses, and friends. We don't often reflect on all of those relationships, but loss allows us an opportunity to do that. If we allow that process to unfold, instead of shutting out certain feelings, we grow and heal." By experiencing their grief, very sad men learn to live again.

For example, Carl Gruener, the president of a business and technical school, paid attention to his pain and gained new perspective on his divorce that contributed toward his healing. "When my marriage fell apart," he recalled, "I felt like a total failure. I died. When we first separated, I felt terrible. It wasn't too bad when the weather was nice, but I dreaded Thanksgiving. Yet the holidays came and went, and I was still alive. In retrospect, they were the most peaceful holidays I had in years. I finally realized that peace was worth everything. Living alone, seeing the children, and going out wasn't that bad after a while."

Grief and Time

The rhythm of the seasons helped Carl Gruener to understand that mourning is a process that takes time. Allowing himself permission to grieve, he changed his perspective on celebrating the holidays and consequently reunited with his children and himself. Ex-husbands free themselves from grief by first accepting it as normal—never an easy task. To heal themselves, they need to keep confronting it affirmatively.

The time required to grow and heal from the grief resulting from divorce is uncertain. After about three months, friends are usually impatient, urging an ex-husband to "snap out of it," or accusing him of "wallowing in self-pity." If this is the only message friends are giving, it is time for a divorced man to be with people who know better. Nonetheless, the process of recovery is generally longer than anyone would hope—some psychologists say a minimum of two years. It is not that a man is hurting all of that time, but he may need that time period to work out all of his feelings. Most concur, however, that the grief process requires at least a year of steady work, generally citing the first anniversary of the divorce as a promising turning point.

No man whom I interviewed for this book treated his marriage as an interruption in his life that left him unchanged. Because divorce, even an amicable one, provokes a profound sense of loss, therapists acknowledge that an ex-husband ought to mourn this loss before entering into a committed relationship with another woman. The point of concentrating on one's pain is not to keep it active, however. The divorced man will simply become more objective about his role in the break-up of his marriage and avoid entering into other destructive relationships. Basically, if a former husband does not learn what needs he had that caused him to enter into a marriage that ended in divorce, he risks marrying a woman who has the same traits and repeating the same scenario.

"As soon as possible after separation," author Douglas Gillette commented to me, "men somehow or other need to go into their inner world. If they identify their grief, go through it, and give it up, they are more likely to understand why the marriage ended."

Therapist Terrance O'Connor made the same point in different terms: "Men can learn a great deal about their relationships by concentrating on their inner world. They gain skill in understanding that if they do x, then someone is likely to do y." Sadly, men seldom consider their love relationships in this way until after they dissolve. But if a divorced man has not thought about his needs, values, and habits, deciding which to keep and which to change, and has not paid attention to his feelings, he is likely to repeat the same patterns and head toward disaster.

Divorce as New Life

Among the therapists I talked with, Joseph Jastrab viewed divorce from a positive approach, saying that this state is often the crisis that provides men an opportunity to look at themselves reflectively. A nationally recognized psychotherapist from New Palz, New York, who specializes in treating men, he provided a vision of divorce that relieves the associations with death and dying, and instead expresses hope, optimism, and new life.

"We tend to pathologize divorce in our culture, but in retrospect it can be a great gift," Jastrab said. "We recognize pain, but pain is not always a symptom of something wrong, in that it should be stopped. The pain of divorce can be parallel to the pain of birth: it's scary, but you would not stop it. Nothing is wrong. Divorce can be like the birthing process. What may be emerging as a result of this effort is the potential of someone more whole than before. By going through the pain, a man may reunite with his emotional life absent before the crisis, and therefore live a fuller life with a woman as a result."

But courage is required for a divorced man to study himself. After all, popular wisdom holds that he is relishing all of the new privileges of bachelorhood. Friends usually discourage any talk of sadness. Even his attorney may think him cushioned from feeling bereaved and estranged. In fact, by treating divorce as the "dissolution of an economic partnership," an attorney trivializes a client's grief.

But society, in general, allows a divorced man little permission to explore and express his loss. Consequently, he will bury his need to mourn because tears symbolize defeat. But the truth is that they also purify illusions. They free one from continually trying to reconstruct an experience, rewrite the script. Tears can be a cry of triumph. They admit that loss, weakness, error, misunderstanding, change, and mortality are part of the way we are. Tears can purge, forgive, affirm. But for men who are continually forced to recall in themselves the boy with skinned knees who is urged to stand up and shake off the dust "like a man," this message often fails to get through.

Rather than the perpetuation of anger, revenge, guilt, and hostility, the self-knowledge born of grief is the ultimate restorative resource for ex-husbands wanting to chart their way into a future that holds some promise of peace and happiness.

MEN AND THERAPY

"I really don't want to be here, but it seems to be the only place."

Everyman

THE MEN INTERVIEWED FOR *Men on Divorce* verified the observation of family therapists, who say that men, in general, seek professional counseling only when wives or sweethearts figuratively put a gun to their temples. Typically, a newly separated or divorced man will try therapy only as a last resort. To do so means admitting that he hurts and cannot easily reach the source of his pain. Sometimes he spends months in a downward spiral before showing up in a professional office to say, "I really don't want to be here, but it seems to be the only place."

Men are often bewildered by the process involved in finding a therapist or counselor specializing in divorce. The best reference is from friends who are familiar with a reputable psychologist, psychiatrist, or psychotherapist with whom they have had success. But as Deborah Tannen, Ph.D., pointed out in the book, *You Just Don't Understand*, men traditionally do not talk about personal problems with each other as easily as women do. In lieu of a friend's recommendation, physicians, clergyman, or attorneys can generally make reliable referrals. If an ex-husband has the time and money, it would be advisable for him to do comparative interviews before making a choice.

The most important criterion for him to weigh is whether the therapist applies the principles of bereavement to marital separation and divorce. If not, the divorced man's healing may be cosmetic. Grief is cumulative because each loss reminds us of previous losses. If an ex-husband does not mourn the losses of his marriage, his pain will be compounded when he faces future losses. Therapy can free a man to express his pain, grow from it, and, if necessary, learn to live again.

Judith A. Talbert, a psychotherapist and Manager of Supportive Service for Family Hospice, Mt. Lebanon, Pennsylvania, explained, "Grief from loss is as emotionally painful as a third-degree burn is physically painful. With a burn, any reasonable man knows that healing takes a long time. He would willingly undergo medical procedures to help himself. He would take it easy with himself. But men are slow to seek professional counseling to help them deal with loss. The stereotype of the strong, independent male prevents men from getting help when they most need it. The more tied a man is to rigid definitions of masculine behavior, the less likely he is to seek therapy. Somehow it's a sign of weakness to talk about problems and feelings."

Choosing a therapist is one of the most important decisions anyone can make. M. Scott Peck, M.D., the author of *The Road Not Taken*, offers guidelines in the Afterword of his landmark book—advice that has been much appreciated by many men whom I interviewed.

In addition, Dr. Bruce Barth, editor of the newsletter, *The Talking Stick*, and an experienced therapist, gave me specific advice tailored for men. "A man should choose a therapist as if he were deciding how well he will function with a new person at work. Men are used to sizing up colleagues and competitors, and sorting out phonies," Barth remarked. "They should utilize and depend upon that practical experience. Certainly check out a résumé and credentials at a professional level, but these really don't indicate how you will feel inside. Don't be afraid of using an intuitive measuring stick: How well do you feel when sitting with him or her? How do you feel when the time comes to return on Tuesday afternoon? If you feel okay inside, that you can talk and trust your life story, then the person is probably competent and you will be helped. If you find yourself saying things you don't want to say, this can be a sign of what you need to say."

Barth believes that men often begin therapy for the wrong reasons. "They want to find out whose fault it was that their marriage failed. They treat therapy as trouble-shooters, as if their business or car were not functioning. They know something is wrong, and they are basically problem-solvers. They want to be back on the road after four or five sessions, and not go inward. Basically, they want to know,

'Why did she leave me?' If they know why she left, then they think the hurt will go away.

"If they begin at pain level four, and the pain level reduces to zero, then they go back to life at the point of disruption with a couple of ideas of how they screwed up. They find another wife and pretty soon repeat the previous pattern because they haven't figured out what the pattern is and how to make a significant change. They keep recycling. It's not that women are at fault, but men who haven't thought things through keep choosing the same type of woman. Then they say, 'What dumb luck I have that women just don't work out.' But when their intimate relationships continue to end unhappily, men are also more likely to go into therapy."

Ex-husbands who gain the most from therapy want more than temporary relief. They probe the dynamics of the relationship they had with their wives, and are willing to let go of illusions that the marriage can be saved. Those who work less get worse results. In some cases, healing may be difficult because the presence of the ex-wife is a continual irritant. On the other hand, after divorce, the possibility of reconciliation does exist, so ex-husbands may obsess:

"If only I had acted differently, this might not have happened."

"If I change my behavior, maybe I can have her back."

"If she would just change, we could have another chance."

An ex-husband who thinks in this fashion may best be helped by a professional therapist who will listen to him, accept and respect the uniqueness of his situation, and work with him until he can organize his life and focus on the future.

"I Need Help"

For a husband who has been left by his wife, or blames himself for the failure of his marriage, the major purpose of his therapy is usually the regaining of self-esteem. Such a man typically thinks: "I must not be a very good person because my wife left me." To help him recover self-worth, therapist Joseph Jastrab has said that the first task is to "affirm the beauty and integrity of the part of him asking for help. It's like a room locked up for years, and he has a list of experiences to justify his not entering there ever again. He needs to be reassured that he can respond to the voice that urges, 'I need help.'"

Barry Knoll is an example of an ex-husband who finally said, "I need help," and grew in self-knowledge as a result. As the managing partner of an accounting firm, Barry described himself as "someone who tells others how to take care of their problems." The lowest point in his life occurred when he arrived home from a business trip to find that his wife and two children had moved out.

"Every morning driving to work on the throughway, I'd feel terribly embarrassed. I felt that everyone in the other cars knew that I was separated. This kept up for months. Then I took a short vacation. I wanted time away from the rat race just to think. One morning walking on the beach by myself, I had the illumination that divorce was too bad, but it didn't mean I was a failure as a human being. I still had worth and value. Everything else stemmed from that realization. I know the process of recovery started at that moment, but it was a long time before I came to grips with what that really meant."

The morning after Barry's wife left their home, she arranged for both of them to meet with a retired seminary professor of theology who specialized in marriage counseling. "That was the kindest thing Martha could have done for me," Barry reflected. "She knew I would be shocked to find that she had left. We both went together to see him for several weeks. But our motives were different. Martha was justifying why she left, and I wanted to save the marriage. We were at cross-purposes, and I had to give up the notion that we could reconcile. But through that, I learned that I really wanted to be married. Those were two big breakthroughs for me that came at separate times: I wanted to be married, and I wasn't a bad person simply because I was divorced."

For a year, Barry met twice a week with the professor, whom he called a "very wise man. The sessions helped me to be more objective about myself. I wasn't ready to be married at age 22, even though I was in love. But at age 40, I figured I knew a lot more about what a marriage should be. So I took stock of what I wanted in a wife. My first wife was very dependent on me. I came to realize that I wanted to be married to a particular kind of person—a woman who was independent outside of our relationship. I was going through a frenetic sexual stage. I knew that in the circles I was presently running, I wasn't going to find anyone like that.

"For six months I backed away and didn't have sexual relations. I realized I wanted a relationship with someone independent, and not a woman I could control and consequently lose respect for. Respect is an important issue. In a year I learned it was important to respect a woman as an individual—that I would have a happier marriage if I gave up my need to control. But it was a lot of pain and suffering before I got to this point."

Barry has been happily married for five years to an "independent woman" who is the development director for a city ballet company. Furthermore, they have blended their two families of teenagers.

"Maybe I'm not a first-class feminist," Barry said, "but I happen to be more comfortable and far less afraid of independent women. But if I hadn't had the conversation that I did for over a year with my professor friend, I would never have gotten here."

The temptation for men with successful careers is to try to recover from divorce on their own. After all, men have been taught to hang tough and go it alone. "It's a real leap, it's a very hard thing to ask for professional help," Barry Knoll sympathized. Consequently, when a man is mismatched with his first psychiatrist, psychologist, or psychotherapist, he is often reluctant to try another. Yet, a bad experience ought to help him define the person with whom he can best communicate. Furthermore, it can help him to decide his choice of support: counseling, therapy, or psychoanalysis.

For example, after realizing that he and Martha had separate agendas in their joint counseling sessions with the seminary professor, Barry began to see a psychiatrist instead. He soon returned to the minister, however, with whom he felt "more comfortable." Barry appreciated that the minister helped him to articulate a philosophy of life. Without imposing his own beliefs, he helped Barry search within himself for the basis of his values.

In choosing psychological support, a divorced man needs to be certain that a therapist or counselor will be open to him, and appreciate divorce as a personal crisis that he must be free to come to terms with. If a man struggling with the repercussions of divorce feels manipulated by a therapist's either rigid or avant-garde views, he should find another one whose basic values are agreeable with his. For example, if a father has custody of his children, but is anxious about his responsibilities as a single parent, he should not connect with a therapist who is biased against a man's assuming this role.

Various types of professionals are able to help a man work through his problems after divorce. Men and women in the clergy are often sources of great comfort. An ex-husband must take the first step himself, however, in recognizing his need to talk with someone who has the ability to listen—someone whom he can trust to guide him through his inner world and redirect his efforts to pursue effective patterns of living. At its best, therapy provides a safe place for a divorced man to focus on himself when he feels unsettled and his world is shaken. But whatever psychological support he elects, ultimately an ex-husband is the one responsible for finding a basis for his future choices.

One Man's Recovery

Al Gundelberg, the general manager of a cable television station, is recognizable as an ex-husband who benefited from therapy after delaying it as long as possible. For years, he coped with his wife's addiction to drugs and alcohol, not to mention her one-night stands with men she would invite into their home. The issue was forced only when his wife unexpectedly left with their two young children. He returned home one evening after the six o'clock news to face a house cleared of furniture, possessions, and credit cards. "At that moment," Al said, "I felt only relief."

Knowing his response must seem unusual, he explained, "For three years I was barely a tenant, hardly a roommate. I stayed because I wanted to hold the family together. I wanted to cling. After our son was born, I had been banished from the bedroom and slept in the basement family room. When Arlene left, I had the whole house. Everything was gone, but so was the tension. The quiet, the relief, the peace was like a vacation. But the initial euphoria soon disappeared. I had very grim days. Everything I had wanted in life had died. I was Fred Flintstone: I had wanted the house with the picket fence, the whole works. I had worked 15 hard years, and everything I had believed in was trashed. I really thought I might die. I was worried that I was willing myself to die. I just sat. I realized I had to do something to rescue myself. I realized I had a choice. I could either pull myself together or die.

"So I went through the house, which had only odds and ends, and put everything in one room. That made me realize that I was picked clean, but I wasn't down to the bare bones. I painted the other rooms. They looked nice and sparkled. I had made some change, and it felt great. I decided to give myself time. I stayed home from October through February—saved money, and learned to dance by watching rented videos. I didn't do that to meet somebody, but I wanted to focus on something, learn something that would not be mentally taxing. The idea that after divorce a bachelor is loose in the world is silly. He's back in the sixties where he left off. I ate potatoes for six months, exercised, lost weight, and scrupulously maintained my relationship with my kids. I was desperate to get on a reasonable track.

"In the spring I emerged. I shaved my beard as a symbol. I was recalcitrant about it, but I started therapy. I felt so sad. The therapist told me I had reason to be sad because I had been wronged. I needed that reassurance. It's good to hear an outside voice say, 'Yes, you have been wronged, and you are a good guy.' Therapy helped me to see the whole picture."

Because of his wife's abuse of their children, the court awarded custody to Al. Each year Al still marks the anniversary of when Kelly (now 20) and Bud (now 16) came to live with him. "Friends always know what we'll be doing on January 23—eating cake. We keep the day sacrosanct," Al laughed merrily, before giving me a favorite recipe for roasting chicken as we said good-bye.

Creative Support Systems

While men reluctantly request counseling or therapy, they often grow dependent upon their therapist once they have established trust. "You are the one to save me," is the way therapist Joseph Jaspers describes their thinking. "When I hear this, I say, 'Unless you are able to find a creative support system in addition to me, you cannot come back because I can't help you at all.'"

Jaspers suggested to me that a creative support system has many forms. It can be an informal network of sympathetic friends who listen while simultaneously encouraging a divorced man to be honest about facing his pain. More often, it means an organized group of men, or men and women, who are at various stages in the cycle of divorce. They meet to explain, discuss, and develop insight into their experiences of separation and divorce. They gain strength, confidence, and inspiration from each other so that they can heal and redirect their lives. Their sessions may or may not be facilitated by a professional therapist.

Carol Randolph, the founder and executive director of New Beginnings, Inc., Silver Spring, Maryland, one of the most successful divorce support groups in the United States, explained, "Men are very reluctant about joining support groups, and look instead for a partner." She began New Beginnings by placing an ad in the September 1979 *Washingtonian* for a meeting that attracted nine persons. Since then, the membership has grown to 1,200, ranging in age from the late twenties to late sixties, with the members being approximately 60 percent female and 40 percent male.

Meetings are scheduled in members' homes, in groups of 15 to 20, throughout the Washington, D.C. metropolitan area, Maryland, and Virginia. Discussion topics include coping with initial feelings of rejection, aloneness, and anger; interacting with a former spouse, children, friends, and families of both partners; the singles scene; and building new relationship skills. Supplementing the small mutual support groups are monthly meetings where experts speak on topics covering legal procedures, financial management, self-esteem, stress reduction, and communication.

Once they join a mutual support group, such as New Beginnings, men are often surprised at how their lives change for the better. Bruce Sauer is one of them.

After 24 years of marriage, Bruce and Gail Sauer were in family counseling together. Five months prior to their separation, their psychologist strongly advised Bruce to join a separation group. Still blind to the signals that his marriage was headed for divorce court, Bruce refused the suggestion. But when his wife made an appointment with an attorney, Bruce checked into H.E.A.R.T. (Helping Each Other Accept Change, Resume Life, and Trust Again), a divorce support group in Pittsburgh. At his first meeting, Bruce remembers imploring the group to tell him something to tell my wife so that his marriage wouldn't disintegrate.

Bruce recalled, "I was there to get quick answers. I tuned into the support group when I finally realized that my marriage was hopeless and couldn't be saved. I became more concerned with how to pick up the pieces and go on. The support group was largely women. I heard women's problems where husbands were cheating. My wife and I didn't cheat on each other; incompatibility was our problem. So at first I couldn't get much out of it. But gradually I began to realize that women were not much different from me. They hurt and were going through pain. That was our bond."

Bruce continued, "Without support, it's like being in a room that's totally black, with black walls, no light, and void of furniture. You can't see to touch the walls or any person. I wanted someone to listen to me and talk to me. I did not miss a meeting. Whether I was feeling up or depressed, I still felt I had to attend. The support group gave me a platform. I needed to talk. I was angry and needed to tell someone. I was damn mad. The last words of my wife to me were 'Get a life, Bruce. You're a good person, but I don't love you. Get a life.'

"I took her advice," Bruce explained. "I wanted to prove to her that I could exist, and that I could find out who I am. The support group helped me to see that I'm not a bad guy. I had thought our marriage had deteriorated just because of me, that I had full responsibility for destroying the marriage. But that wasn't the case. I learned that I was okay, and that others liked me, too. Now I'm much happier out of the marriage than in it. I could not have said that a year ago. When I began with the support group, I wanted Gail back under any conditions. But now I see our marriage would not have worked and could never be formulated on the basis we had."

Bruce is the general manager of a trucking company. He explained, "I work in a very masculine environment where I had little satisfaction in trying to communicate. I had to be clandestine about getting a divorce. When the divorce was granted, a man I work with said he had seen my name in the paper. I said, 'Yes. I've divorced.' That was about it. Support groups bring relief. It's like getting on an airplane and talking because you'll never see the person again. But with support groups, you keep going back. Sometimes you get nothing, but it's a building-block process. The support group gave me back my worth. And I didn't have to pay a therapist or counselor. If you can't pay a therapist, support groups are no cost, or limited cost, and are great. But the key is being patient in finding the right support group for yourself."

H.E.A.R.T. was the right place for Bruce because he liked the fact that a trained professional facilitated the discussion and offered positive suggestions for changing behavior patterns. When support groups are left on their own, they sometimes have difficulty moving away from anger. Furthermore, home remedies for dealing with psychological pain can be damaging.

Bruce's experience represented the positive advantages of a support group composed of men and women. As Carol Randolph, executive director of New Beginnings, said to me, "They offer a balance of perspective that prevents discussion from degenerating into 'all men are rotten,' or 'no woman can be trusted.'" In 1979, Randolph began New Beginnings when she realized that most support services were for divorced women with children, but that divorced women without children were overlooked. At first, her groups were segregated according to gender, but now she believes in bringing men and women together. "It's important to the healing process to see the hurt of the opposite sex, who can also feel sadness and pain."

For similar reasons, Patricia Jameson began H.E.A.R.T. after feeling isolated when she divorced 12 years ago. She agreed with Randolph's assessment about mixed groups, and offered a humorous insight: "At the beginning, men and women dump their garbage on each other. A man might remark, 'That's just what my wife would say. You remind me of her; in fact, you look like her.' A woman might say, 'You're just like my husband.' But in that interaction," Jameson contended, "a man and woman get to confront and understand in a group what they didn't work out in their private relationship. The group provides a safe environment. They really can't kill each other, but by listening, they enter into each other's lives.

"When a man starts talking about how he feels, a woman might hear her husband's story, and vice versa. Gradually, the stress begins to lessen, and they are able to look at the interpersonal patterns in their marriages, and see how they participated in creating the conflict. Men and women then come to see each other as individuals who hurt, care, and have feelings. They begin to see each other as good people who have value, and can go on with their gifts and talents."

Men join divorce support groups like H.E.A.R.T. and New Beginnings only when they are ready to talk about their feelings, and want to have a fuller understanding of why their marriages ended in divorce. "A man doesn't suddenly decide to attend a group meeting," Jameson pointed out. "It's after some process, usually after realizing that he doesn't really have anyone to talk to. He's ready to admit that he needs help and has to do something for himself. It takes a great deal for a man to participate in group-talk because it's a feminine way of interaction. Women for years have had coffee and talked about interpersonal issues. But when men come together, they talk about safe things—sports, golf—not their interior life."

The research of Deborah Tannen has brought popular attention to the complexities of communication differences between men and women. Gaining self-affirmation through open discussion is counter to how both genders have expected men to behave. Men are not practiced in expressing their vulnerability, nor are they certain that they will receive a sympathetic response if they reveal how they truly feel. Consequently, each time a man attends a meeting of a divorce support group, he puts himself on the line.

Support Groups for Men

For this reason, many therapists favor a men's group instead of one composed of men and women. "After a divorce, a man can get lost in his own head by going into a closet or sitting in a bar," said therapist Terrance O'Connor, who sees men's support groups as "safe places for ex-husbands to work out their emotions. If men are with women, they can fall back into a dependent mode. But no one is going to be Mommy in a men's group. Behavior that is nurturing and gentle has to come from men. Male nurturance is different. A man will say, 'You jerk, look at what you did.' If men get nurturance from each other, it breaks the cycle that men have to be dependent upon a wife or girlfriend to interpret and express their feelings. When a divorced man is then ready to resume a relationship with a woman, he doesn't burden her to take care of all of his emotional needs on demand."

Advocates of men's groups protest the stereotype that they are havens for women-bashing. Those favoring a separatist approach are convinced that listening to the stories of other men provides a deeper identification for ex-husbands than hearing the stories of women. With women present, they are more likely to maintain a front of being brave, strong, and silent. They are more apt to hide their fears and concerns. In the presence of men, they gain perspective on the masculine experience of divorce, but still have room to reflect freely on their own unique situation. They may also feel more free in venting anger and sadness.

One man admitted having attended ten sessions of a men's group, however, before feeling comfortable enough to say a word. He confessed, "It took me a while before I realized I could be emotionally open with men and trust them. The first time I actually said what I was most afraid to say, I knew I was dealing more positively with my own fears. Then I realized the world hadn't come to an end because I had said it. I even got approval." This approbation is the reversal of the affirmation that men generally give each other for being stoical, aggressive, and competitive. Instead, they share permission to be open and responsive to each other.

Attorney Ed Honnold, founder of the Men's Collective in Washington, D.C., gave me his definition of a constructive group: "It first supports a man's worth and then challenges him to question and examine himself and his own unfinished emotional business. It helps him to see the personal factors that have contributed to the breakdown of the marriage so that he won't enter into another unworkable relationship. I think this kind of introspection is best accomplished with other men.

A support group isn't a place to find another woman, but it can provide a holding pattern for men in a traumatic situation."

For example, men in a divorce support group often help each other to see patterns of relationship addiction. Men in each other's company create a community that focuses on an ex-husband's pain, but encourages him to appreciate that his healing will be achieved through self-understanding, not a premature marriage. After separation and divorce, a man frequently commits himself to a woman prematurely because he has no other outlet for expressing how he feels. He is not comfortable telling male friends that he hurts.

On the other hand, men in a divorce support group act as a mutual tracking station, helping each other to sort out their problems before starting a serious romantic relationship. "I don't agree that a man should take two years away from women and be fallow," said therapist Terrance O'Connor. "The important thing is that he allow himself a period of time to be introspective." Furthermore, O'Connor thinks that men's support groups affirm a masculine identity while helping men to value intimacy and express their sadness. He said that the first concern of a strong support group is to help each member come to self-understanding. Their focus is to help members avoid actions and situations that will cause further pain and destruction to themselves and others.

Based on her experience as a therapist, Kim Underwood agreed with O'Connor about the value of men's support groups, and commented, "The worst thing for a man is to think that he can't be true to his own gender but must learn his feelings from a woman. If he must take lessons from a women, he worries that he will *be* like a woman."

Men and Women as Abusers

Divorced men who are wife-abusers cannot even imagine being part of a group that would include women. Their journey to recovery is particularly difficult. "There would be too much blocking to acknowledge the extent of the damage if women were there," said Carl Bates, an admitted wife-abuser. More helpful to him than therapy or marriage counseling was his participation in a group that focused on behavior modification, facilitated by a psychologist specializing in abuse. The problem is that not enough programs exist across the country for men who want counseling for violent behavior.

Carl signed a six-month contract with The Second Step Program, a support group in southwestern Pennsylvania. Groups meet weekly, composed of six or eight men willing to recognize themselves as abusers—a significant first step.

Carl described the program as he experienced it. "As an initial exercise, participants have to describe the last time they were abusive, in slow-action. At first they might say, 'Oh, and then she fell down.' But the role-playing slows down second by second, moment by moment, to a freeze-frame when they finally say, 'Then I hit her.' It's a very powerful exercise. A man has to recreate and come to terms with what he has done. It's very painful because men who never have cried can be in uncontrollable pain when they actually confront their abuse. The therapist asks the vulnerable question: 'How did she react?' The abuser has to pay attention, listen, and recall. Finally, he has to come to terms with how his wife must have felt. The key point is that the abuser has to say 'I am an abuser.' On entering the program, those words are usually impossible."

Carl further remarked, "In these sessions, I have seen men sometimes describe for the first time how they were sexually or physically abused as children. They can be executives or welfare recipients, but their suffering is enormous. It's the most profound experience I've ever had with other individuals."

Marriages are sometimes saved through programs like The Second Step, or Victim Services in New York City. But men whose marriages have already ended in divorce at least find solace in having a better understanding of negative influences on their behavior, and consequently how to control them. Some feel more confident about entering into another relationship with a woman as a result of being able to recognize their own early warning signs toward abusiveness. They are taught how to slow the action, and call for support when the signals reappear.

Public awareness has grown regarding male physical abuse against women and children. Treatment and shelters for battered women and children must be guaranteed. But, as Murray A. Strauss and Richard Gelles point out in *Physical Violence in American Families*, "Victims need and deserve help in dealing with the emotional trauma of the abuse; and perpetrators need help to learn to change their violent behaviors." Yet, programs for abusive men are scarce across the country and are seldom financially secure.

Men wanting to change their abusive behavior patterns generally feel great shame. But husbands who are victims of physical and verbal abuse also deal with shame. More than the public likes to think, women, according to research by Straus and Gelles, "initiate violence about as often as men . . . casting doubt on the notion that assaults by women on their partners primarily are acts of self-defense or retaliation."

The intent of *Men on Divorce* is to relate the stories of men who have experienced divorce, not to supply conclusive empirical evidence regarding any related complex issue. But personal narratives can be the basis for quantitative research. Two men out of the 45 I interviewed described how they were physically abused by their wives. They told me that they avoided retaliation for fear that their superior strength could cause irreparable damage or even death. Nonetheless, when enduring physical attacks, they felt an obligation to protect their wives and save their marriages.

One man referred to himself as being "abused" by his wife's unrelenting verbal assaults. Other men claimed to have absorbed similar insults but did not characterize themselves as having been abused. This type of domestic violence is an issue that needs to be addressed without fear that such research betrays the cause of battered women and children.

Codependency Groups

Codependency groups also offer possibilities for recovering from the loss of divorce. Adult Children of Divorce (which has become more broad in its focus), Al-Anon, and Overeaters Anonymous provide opportunities for self-reflection. From 12-step programs, men often move into psychotherapy. The irony is that couples may divorce because of the support of such programs. After becoming sober through Alcoholics Anonymous, for example, a person's recovery process may include insights that lead to the end of the marriage.

As a culture, we do not foster the attitude that men suffer domestic conflict or can be emotionally incapacitated after divorce. In response, divorced men neither admit their feelings nor know how to deal with them. As a result, they are reluctant to enter into therapy or explore other therapeutic options.

Confronting the Truth

Our cultural myth is that men sail right through the divorce process, or, if troubled, find quick redemption in the arms of a compliant woman. After interviewing 45 ex-husbands, I am convinced that our myth makes magic out of their true stories. For months, sometimes years, after divorce, ex-husbands are often still in pain.

Dr. Ralph P. Brooks, a clinical psychologist and Episcopalian priest specializing in divorce, contends that "many people who get divorced don't really get divorced. They remain intertwined in each other's emotions and psyches. Resentments can remain unresolved. There can be a lot of basic competitiveness and comparing jealousies. A good day in the ex-mate's life can become a bad day for me. It's all very much beyond the range of the logical, rational, and objective fact. It's more in the realm of deep and primitive attachments. Divorce is an emotionally exhausting experience, and men don't always know how to deal with that part of it."

An ex-husband makes positive changes in his life only after confronting the truth of why his marriage ended. He needs to resolve anger and guilt, accept himself, and feel valued. This approval is most likely to occur in a professional therapeutic relationship or within a support situation where he achieves confidence and self-understanding. Husbands needing to regain their balance do so after a sustained period of hard introspection. The recovery from divorce is a chaotic journey, not a predictable tour with a planned itinerary. Healing is the result of concentrated effort, not miracles.

PRACTICAL ADVICE
FOR HEALING

"I know I can recover naturally, find happiness,
if I don't rush things and screw it up."

—Stephen Marshall, age 35

EX-HUSBANDS WHO RECOVER from the pain of divorce advise men to concentrate on their inner space with the same attention they give to negotiations in their attorney's office. A legal divorce is the definitive outcome of a step-by-step court process. But the emotional recovery from divorce is spiral, not linear. No amount of conceptual knowledge about divorce will relieve an ex-husband's grief, guilt, anger, or loneliness. By concentrating solely on the legal process of his divorce, he detaches himself from understanding divorce as a personal crisis.

A man may not need to turn to professional counseling during separation and divorce, but because divorce means loss, it is in his best interest to spend time gaining a clearer understanding of himself and how he wants to refocus his life.

Many ways exist for an ex-husband to help himself. Keeping a journal is highly recommended as a practical way for men in the cycle of divorce to release their thoughts and feelings, ponder their needs, and discover patterns to their behavior. By keeping a journal, a man becomes his own friend. Therapist Joseph Jastrab told me that he advises private writing because "it allows a man to tell his psyche that he is serious, that he's willing to listen to his own story. A journal really opens up his schedule, allows time for dealing with his pain, which he could easily ignore by filling his hours with work and diversionary activities."

A man who keeps a journal also has the advantage of controlling the amount of pain he wants to bear at a given time. He need not write in it every day, for example. He can put it aside for a while and return to it when he is ready. A diary often helps a former husband to write down things that in retrospect he wish he had said to his wife. It provides a way of expressing sorrow, guilt, and anger. Moreover, a journal is a good listener, for it will not register boredom from hearing the same stories repeated. To gain perspective on incidents that occurred between him and his wife, it is not unusual for an ex-husband to repeat himself. In my interviews, for example, I often heard about a particular episode more than once within the same session.

A journal provides opportunities for a divorced man to explore memories from earlier days, even before his marriage. Revisiting a younger self is often a therapeutic adventure, allowing him to see the complex reasons behind the choices that he made. By writing in a journal and then placing it aside or locking it away, an ex-husband has a tangible symbol of measuring his progress and putting his divorce behind him. One man burned his journal when he was finally able to stop viewing himself as a failure and was ready to move on.

A journal is also a fine place for musing over dreams. It is possible to pay attention to them without necessarily being schooled in dream interpretation. Writing about dreams while they are still vivid allows a man another way to listen to himself that moves beyond logic. For example, one man recalled making a list of people to inform that he and his wife were divorcing. He thought he could easily rejoin the mainstream of life, until he had a dream of being surrounded by people, pointing fingers at him. Writing in his journal about the implications of the dream, he knew he could not only count on his friends for moral support, and sought professional counseling.

Personal writing can also take the form of unmailed letters. This strategy proved effective for a husband who raged with anger when his wife filed for divorce. Although their marriage was not compatible, he never thought it would end. In writing letters to her in which he reviewed their life together, he discovered how selective his hearing had been. As he wrote, he heard echoes of their serious disagreements, and acknowledged for the first time his denial of what she had been saying to him about her unhappiness and what they had to change in their relationship. The marriage was not saved, but the process of writing unmailed letters lessened his hostility and helped him to accept his share of blame.

Masculine Mysteries

In whatever way a man chooses to be introspective about the loss of his marriage, he may unexpectedly meet the boy he left behind in his childhood during the process. A man who was dependent on his wife may feel emotionally immature and lonely without her to take care of him. In such cases, Joseph Jastrab urges men to "comfort the boy and really become father to that part of you that wants attention and feels forlorn." As an example, he suggests that a man buy himself whatever he enjoyed as a child, whether it be a plastic whistle, a stick of bubblegum, or a baseball. If a father gives a young son a simple gift, it is a sign of his love. The son is happy, and the father expects nothing in return.

Similarly, Jastrab points out, when an adult man gives himself bubblegum or a baseball, he responds to the needs of the inner boy and acknowledges the friendship he has for himself. The token makes the respect he has for the crisis he is going through more visible. Eventually, he is able to give himself other gifts that are nurturing and healing, such as taking off a Saturday to walk in the woods. His awareness deepens about nourishing his spiritual life, the center of his worth and being, rather than the world of work and commerce. Divorce then becomes an opportunity for him to reach a new level of integrated maturity, which balances being and doing.

Taking time for solitude is crucial for a man going through the crisis of divorce. As a positive way of thinking about masculine identity, Douglas Gillette, author of *King, Warrior, Magician, Lover*, suggested to me that ex-husbands read the autobiographies and biographies of men.

"Certainly a man can go through a divorce without therapy," he contended, "but somehow or other he has to be willing to go into his feelings and the world of masculine mysteries, and reading about men's lives can help him to do that." A first-person narrator's description of how he shaped choices for himself is a possible model for men searching for ways to redirect their lives. Biographies that reveal the complex interpersonal relationships in men's lives may also help ex-husbands to interpret their own experiences in terms of past, present, and future.

For example, a man I interviewed benefited greatly from reading biographies of the Trappist monk Thomas Merton, as well as his autobiographical writings and journals. Merton inspired him to focus on his spiritual life, long neglected by his efforts to advance in his career and financially support a large family. By meditating on Merton, he found coherence to his life. He began to affirm his own goodness and find joy in the simple pleasures of the moment. After years of feeling demeaned by his wife, he once more valued himself and his gifts. Through Merton's example, he also grew in his capacity for expressing sympathy and authentic concern for others. He was ready to step into the future.

Ed Honnold, the founder of the Men's Council of Washington, believes that men are just now coming to realize that they do not want to continue in the same patterns of behavior that "make a man a man: keeping the wolf from the door; keeping fires burning and the boundaries safe." On the other hand, the blurred edges between gender roles make many men uncomfortable as they try to decide what it is about men that is not like women. Men want to live out a more sensitive masculinity, but the old rules for manliness were easier to follow. Men's councils, collectives, and resource centers existing across the United States sponsor events for men to share their thoughts and experiences on a broad range of issues that men traditionally do not talk about with each other—such as intimacy, grief, love, tears, homophobia, male myths, spirituality, and a very popular topic—father-son relationships.

The workshops, seminars, lectures, and special-interest sessions sponsored by men's collectives allow men an opportunity to open up emotionally and explore their sense of self. For example, the mission of the Twin Cities Men's Center (TCMC) in Minneapolis, one of the oldest in the United States founded in 1976, is "to provide resources for men seeking to grow in body, mind, and spirit. TCMC offers a variety of educational forums, peer-support groups, and other activities to foster emotional, intellectual, and spiritual growth."

Typically included in TCMC's monthly calendar of events are presentations by professionals on issues such as "Men Breaking Silence to End Men's Violence"; "Fathers and Daughters"; "Why Men Die Eight Years Younger than Women"; "Men, Work, and Play"; "Moving Out of Our Co-Dependence and Into Healthier Relationships"; and "Writing as a Journey of Discovery." Each night the Center is busy with support groups on divorce, uncoupling, and gay issues. As a special event, the Men's Center sponsors a biannual conference that attracts a national audience. In "Men Nurturing Men," an essay in the *Networker* (May/June 1990), Dr.Terrance O'Connor described the rewards of participating in one of the many weekly meetings sponsored by the Men's Council of Washington:

> We begin to lay out our fears and our personal dilemmas as if we were laying down armfuls of wood we have carried for too long. As the weeks go on, our cares roll out . . . Some of us cry, perhaps for the first time in front of other men. The themes repeat: love, work, Dad. It is amazing not to be alone with this. An exhilaration begins to rise with the realization that we are experiencing a trust and understanding that is different than any we have experienced with women. It has something to do with intimacy without fear of dependence . . . .

Practical Suggestions

Hundreds of events similar to the one O'Connor described in Washington are available nationwide. A calendar of events is listed, for example, in *The Talking Stick*, a quarterly newsletter about men, edited by Bruce W. Barth. *Wingspan: A Journal of the Male Spirit*, an international quarterly published by Dick Halloran, has the widest circulation of publications in the men's movement. It lists a resource directory and a calendar of events throughout the country, plus essays and book reviews.

Books that ex-husbands and therapists whom I interviewed particularly recommended as being helpful include: *Crazy Time: Surviving Divorce*, by Abigail Trafford; *Fire in the Belly: On Being A Man*, by

Sam Keen; *Intimate Strangers*, by Lillian B. Rubin; *Iron John: A Book About Men*, by Robert Bly; *King, Warrior, Magician, Lover,* by Robert Moore and Douglas Gillette; *Men and Divorce,* by Michael F. Myer; *Men and Friendship,* by Stuart Miller; *Men Talk: How Men Really Feel About Women; Sex, Relationships and Themselves* by Alvin Baraff; and *To Be a Man: In Search of the Deep Masculine*, edited by Keith Thompson. Divorced men repeatedly refer to the value of *The Road Less Traveled: A New Psychology of Love, Traditional Values and Spiritual Growth* by M. Scott Peck, M.D.

Whatever practical means a man chooses to help himself recover from divorce—reading, writing, meditating, or attending seminars on men's issues—it is a time for him to learn about himself, to concentrate on what he feels and why. This is hard to do at the beginning of the divorce process when contradictory feelings of guilt, anger, hurt, and self-pity are so strong.

Bereavement specialists offer a number of realistic ways for coping positively with these conflicting emotions, for they agree that a man ought to express the emotions he is feeling because repressing them only further dissipates his energy.

For example, if a man is sad and wants to cry about his marriage but cannot, therapist Cathleen Fanslow-Brunjes recommends renting a video such as *Terms of Endearment,* and watching it by himself. Leafing quietly through family photograph albums is also a way to unleash pent-up sorrow. If he is angry, Fanslow-Brunjes suggests turning up the radio or screaming in the shower. If he punches a bag or rips egg cartons and beats them with a wooden spoon, he is releasing hostility, not going crazy. In a gentler way, one man, Fanslow-Brunjes recalls, learned to crewel and inundated all of his friends with gifts of fancy pillowcases, napkins, and tablecloths.

A newly separated or divorced man may feel sad at particular times of the day, such as early evening when he usually arrives home from work. If this is so, he can schedule other activities for that time that require physical exertion, such as tennis, racquetball, handball, or swimming. He can join a community or office softball team. Exercise in the evening also encourages a sense of well-being that may contribute to better sleeping.

Sundays, holidays, and anniversaries are often difficult for estranged husbands. If so, those days might be filled with volunteer work in hospitals, with youth groups, or in soup kitchens. Helping others through their loneliness is a way of shedding light on one's own problems.

This is also a time, however, when a hurting man needs to appreciate his virtues. He can make a list of his good points and his accomplishments: the fact that he is a team player at work or the office, a loyal brother, a caring father, a talented woodcarver. This list may visually represent to him that he is indeed a good person, and that his failings exist among many positive traits. Knowing that he can identify his flaws, he may stop feeling burdened by personal failure and begin to act on those things that he can do to improve.

During separation and divorce, when a man centers on finanacial and legal matters, he often forgets his health. Recovery from divorce includes attention to a healthful diet and adequate rest. Alcohol and endless hours of ESPN are not effective anodynes for masking pain.

A safer way of relieving stress and promoting healing is Therapeutic Touch, a treatment developed in the early 1970s by Dolores Krieger, Ph.D., R.N., a professor at New York University. Therapuetic Touch is currently practiced by over 20,000 licensed practitioners throughout the United States, Canada, and around the world.

A therapeutic touch treatment is individualized and usually does not exceed 30 minutes. Without undressing, the patient sits in a chair or reclines while a practitioner passes his or her hands (holding them two to four inches away) over the entire body, in order to assess the condition of the human energy field. The practitioner then uses rhythmical, sweeping motions with the hands that promote relaxation and a sense of comfort. During a treatment, signs of tension release, such as perspiration, crying, physical relaxation, and a decrease in heart rate can be detected.

Above all, when a man going through divorce feels unloved, guilty, or angry, he needs to treat himself physically and emotionally with patience and care. This includes accepting the help of others willing to listen sympathetically to his story. But when men want sympathy, they frequently turn to women. Consequently, a divorced man often enters into a new, long-term codependent relationship before he truly understands why his marriage did not last.

If he does not give himself time to mourn his disappointment or exorcise the need to blame, unresolved guilt and anger may haunt his future. Moreover, a surrogate wife who assumes his emotional "dirty work" may only prepare him for marriage with another woman, while she is left with memories. As a rule of thumb, therapists recommend that a man wait at least a year after his divorce is final to think seriously about remarrying.

Former husbands who are most positive about their present lives advise men to begin the journey toward recovery with themselves. The solitary introspection that they recommend is not a self-serving, self-indulgent, self-pitying exercise. But they believe that divorced men can benefit from their loneliness if they use the time to become more conscious of their inner resources. They urge men not to give up on themselves by denying their pain with a frenetic lifestyle or escaping from it via alcohol or drugs. They advise living through the pain and taking honest steps for understanding why it is there. With his new insight, a divorced man is less apt to enter into a relationship where the pain is likely to return.

This is a difficult message for a newly separated man to hear. No one understands this more than many of the ex-husbands I talked with for this book. Yet their emphasis is on hope.

For example, a man who described himself as stumbling through a "black tunnel" after his divorce, told me his story in order "to reach another man to say you can make it. You can make it and be happy." Our customary, easy assumption is that men do not suffer from the effects of divorce, when, in fact, getting through an ordinary day is often an act of faith.

THE PROBLEM WITH FRIENDS

"My male friends would say, 'Oh, you just need to get laid and you'll get over it.'"

—Jeb Turnbull, journalist, age 28

DIVORCE IS A COMMON OCCURRENCE, but few people really know how to treat a newly separated or divorced man. Members of his family and friends often contribute to his loneliness, just at the time when he most needs them.

Many of the men I interviewed were disappointed, some bitterly, by the insensitive or awkward responses of friends and families. The examples of callous remarks that they provided illustrate how one should never react toward a man in the throes of divorce. During this time, he wants compassionate friendship, as opposed to fraternal correction or outright approval. And he should not settle for less.

Roy Anderson illustrated that point. He and his wife, married 15 years, had agreed to a divorce after both had affairs: "I agonized that we had caused each other so much pain. I telephoned both my sister and my best friend. Neither of them really heard me when I told them I was getting a divorce. In a weird way, they began talking about their own lives and how they had coped with similar problems. My friend remarked that if his divorced friends had put the same energy into repairing their relationships, they would have had a better marriage. Then I called my sister, who said I was expecting too much from marriage. That all anyone could expect from it was a friend and an occasional bed partner. Instead of running up the phone bill, she said she'd put her thoughts on tape and send it to me. I didn't speak to either one of them for three months."

Roy cautioned, "A man going through a divorce does not expect his friends to solve his problems. He calls because he is afraid of losing them. When you get that kind of call, the instinct is to think, 'What would I do in his position?' and offer advice. But at that point, just put your arm around the guy because that's what he wants you to do."

In trying to help a friend in pain, a man is more likely to rush forth with solutions to "fix it," when active listening would be a better remedy. To say "yes, what you're going through is terrible," is far more comforting than to counter with "this is what you have to do." Or "let me tell you what happened to me." Sharing experiences is important, but not as the initial response to a man needing affirmation. "Don't try to cheer him up or suggest getting drunk; just listen to him" is the most common advice given by ex-husbands who are hurting.

Male friends do not always help each other move on very easily, though. Jeb Turnbull, 28 years old and single, never thought about this fact until after his six-year relationship ended with a woman he loved. "My male friends would say, 'Oh, you just need to get laid and you'll get over it.' They'd say anything except, 'Really tell me how you feel.' They completely denied that I was experiencing anything but simple regret or horniness. I felt grief but didn't know what to do about it. There was nothing from my male world that I could draw from. With female friends, I had more validation for how I felt kicked in the ribs. But because of the lack of understanding I had from my male friends, I'm now able to say, 'I'm not interested in your *persona*; I want to talk about *you*.' Men have to cope with loneliness in a way that is more productive than sitting in a bar."

Communal Disapproval

Shallow words of comfort offered by good friends only intensify the pain of a grieving man. But his loneliness is compounded when he also feels communal disapproval. The silent criticism of church friends is especially disillusioning and not unusual in the experiences of men with whom I talked. Jerry Fusione is one of them: "I felt like a leper when I went to church after Peggy and I were separated. These were people I had worshipped with for years, but I never heard from them. I had little support from the minister. Quick dividing lines form in social and community groups because people believe they can't associate with both husband and wife. But I didn't expect such polarization at church. There's not much support for husbands in divorce."

Another couple, Carl and Betty Gruener, occupied the same church pew each Sunday of their married life. But the week after their separation, Carl did not know where to sit. Fellow worshippers did not make him feel comfortable about having many choices. He moved across the aisle. Then into the choir loft. Then out the door.

Some husbands who experienced this type of hypocrisy became more responsible for their own spiritual development. Solitude became a time for their self-reflection. But they were most likely to draw their new best friends from among other ex-husbands who knew not to judge their behavior or belittle their pain. When given the opportunity themselves, they became better friends to others in need.

The Best of Friends

For the reasons stated above, divorced men generally know how to help each other better than friends who have not been divorced. They are not as insistent that a man in the process of divorce keep his "chin up." Neither are they quick to suggest with a wink what a great time he must be having. On the contrary, ex-husbands frequently describe feeling inept as they try to start a social life. "I didn't know what to do when I was sprung on the world," said Al Gundelberg, who was divorced nine years ago. He stays active in a divorce support group in order to help other men get through the early stages. He attends meetings, gives out his telephone number, and takes a regular turn on the divorce hotline. But he also listens and supports men and women who are not members because he vividly remembers how he felt when he was in their shoes.

A friend like Al Gundelberg reassures a newly separated or divorced man that others have felt his sorrow, helplessness, restlessness, or turmoil. He offers nonjudgmental understanding and permits a man to express his pent-up emotions. A divorced man need not give up his old friends, but when they do not know how to receive his pain, he needs to find consolation with men who do.

Therapist Joseph Jastrab offered this image to me: "A friend going through divorce is on a sinking raft, and he's best with another man who has also been through the process and can help him to stay with his pain honestly. A man who has gone through divorce knows that facing that pain without fear is the hardest work a man will ever do. It's next to impossible without support." But, if an ex-husband has not examined his own emotional life after divorce, he may not be receptive to a friend in need. Instead, he may feel threatened and back off from a divorced man who is openly grieving.

For example, after his divorce, Al Gundelberg claims to have tried "all that bonding stuff. I talked. I cried. I wasn't posturing. I really opened up. But one-on-one, men maintain a facade with each other. I found I could trust a woman more. There's malespeak I've adopted. When a man asks me how I'm doing, now I say 'great' or grunt 'okay.' If a woman asks, I'm more honest and say, 'I feel a little sad.'"

During his divorce, a man who had lunch daily with the same friends over a period of years never shifted the conversation away from football and the stock market. These friends never suspected that the man's divorce was a trauma for him. Another man, an accountant who had worked for the same firm for 16 years, never talked about his troubles with his partner. "Just once, I talked to a guy I played handball with. But I did confide in a woman ten years older, a wise woman who was like an aunt to me. I still open up more with women in general. It's not that I would not choose to talk to a man, but they just don't respond to feelings."

Women as Safe Friends

Many ex-husbands I interviewed conceded that men are not practiced in developing the kind of friendships where they comfortably seek emotional support from each other. They do not count on men to respond sensitively to their need for understanding. When they want sympathy, they will more often turn to women.

For example, after his separation, Charlie Butler, an artist, valued his women friends more than therapy. "Therapy helped, but it wasn't as crucial as being able to be with friends who let me whine and scream and yell. For about six months, friends allow you to feel sorry for yourself, and say over and over again, 'How could she have done that.' But you can't keep that up in perpetuity.

"Being an artist, I had many women friends of various ages for many years. They were safe because none of us was interested in a romance. In fact, it was a friend, not my therapist, who suggested that I travel West and try to gain a new perspective on my life. That trip was really what turned me around emotionally and inspired me to paint again."

Women allowed Charlie to vent. They compared their experiences of divorce, and said to each other, "Wait till you hear my story." Outside of a therapeutic or structured situation, men are seldom able to call upon each other as freely. Charlie's friendships with women were *safe*, however. It is wiser for a man who needs to heal his spirit to seek friendships with women with whom he is unlikely to have a love affair. Otherwise, in order to ease his loneliness, he may marry prematurely.

Not every ex-husband is as smart, for example, as Roy Anderson in understanding and avoiding the pressure to remarry. He wants to be close to another woman, but consciously avoids getting too involved: "I want someone who is willing to listen and then says, 'I want to tell you about what's going on in my life.' Intimacy right now is what I want more than anything else. But I know intellectually and emotionally that as much as possible I need to work through feelings to forgive my wife and myself before I'll be a safe person to make a commitment."

A questionable axiom asserts that women have been conditioned to value themselves more when they are in a relationship with a man. Similarly, men are socialized to depend upon women to enable their expression of feelings, and, in general, to take care of them. Ex-husbands who relied upon their wives to cook their meals, sort their black socks, take their shirts to the laundry, and keep their social calendars may need marriage more than their ex-wives do.

Furthermore, to have a woman in his life often helps a man feel that he has achieved. A woman becomes the sign of his success. If he is suffering a loss of esteem, an ex-husband can short-circuit his recovery and fall into another bad marriage. Instead of patiently healing and learning from his divorce so that he can make choices about his future, an emotionally scarred man will passively accept that he is incomplete without a partner. Ex-husbands regain self-acceptance by being actively introspective, not helplessly dependent on women. Consequently, while a man after divorce may feel closer bonds with women, the best advice—without second opinions—is to avoid a permanent commitment until he understands why his first marriage did not work. But since ex-husbands say they are more likely to verbalize their heartache with women than with men, they place themselves at early risk.

Side by Side

One of my interviewees, a man who was divorced after 26 years of marriage, said with envy, "It's much easier for a divorced woman to meet a woman friend for dinner and a movie. I wouldn't think to do that with a guy. When guys want companionship, they can only go to sports events together. And it gets lonely."

This does not have to be, according to Paul Lyons, a therapist astute about loss and separation. What is true is that men are more apt to speak about what is happening in their lives while bowling, skiing, sailing, camping, or chopping wood. Unless they have a trusting camaraderie like that between lifetime fishing or golfing buddies, men are slow to unburden themselves. Men traditionally have had to feel safe, Lyons observed, before giving themselves permission to talk about what is hurting them. But the stereotype persists that men are discussing only the game they are playing, the sports event they are watching, or the patio they are building. Men fear, nevertheless, that talking about their feelings with each other means sacrificing their masculine style of friendship of sitting side by side, giving up the game to lounge around and gossip.

However, when men do trust each other in new ways, they describe their satisfaction. For example, a recently divorced man sat at his kitchen table and confided, "The first time in college I was really friends with a guy, he turned out to be gay, and ever since I've backed up from any intimate conversations with men. Now it's really surprised the hell out of me what a help divorced guys have been to me. I'm not afraid anymore to be emotional with a guy. I don't think about it."

An easy remedy does not exist for ex-husbands who shirk opportunities for expressing how they feel because such behavior is unacceptable to their image of masculinity. But just one trusted friend or relative can make life less of an uphill struggle.

When an ex-husband is able to verbalize his heartache, he has a fresh chance for learning how to live with hope. The crucial paradox, however, is that without a friend to listen, he becomes more isolated than ever. The struggle to communicate is dual: the divorced man's need for a listener balances against the listener's need to free himself from responding with bravado or detached advice. When men pull together successfully, their celebrations are not always for victory, but for having the courage to admit how they feel defeated.

Such, then, are the new and demanding terms of male friendship in the nineties: "I'm not interested in your *persona*; I want to talk about *you*."

THE MYSTIQUE OF
CHILD CUSTODY

"Taking my kids back on Sunday nights put me through torture."

—Glenn Argall, health mainenance
executive, age 43

THE FATHERS I talked with for *Men On Divorce* enjoy being dads, but child custody is frightening territory for them. A woman in the process of divorce is usually at risk about the terms of her financial settlement. A man is most vulnerable about child custody arrangements. It is his blind spot.

When I made this observation to David L. Levy, Esq., Founder and President of the National Council for Children's Rights in Washington, D.C., he agreed.

"Access to children is the most perplexing issue with men and divorce across the United States," he commented. "During marriage, fathers see themselves as important, but after divorce, they fear slipping into obscurity. If there is an accident on the road, we stop to help. But no one stops to help a man going through divorce, and he does not want to lose meaningful contact with his children."

In the midst of the public effort to call attention to deadbeat dads who do not maintain ties with their families, we have lost sight of fathers who enjoy their role and want to be lovingly involved in their children's lives. Throughout my interviews, I often heard men say, "If I had my way to write the script, I'd get married once and watch the kids go off to college. But that didn't happen. To do it over again, I wouldn't have married her. But I love my kids. That's what really hurts."

Glenn Argall, president of an HMO, never had any sympathy for fathers who left their children until he experienced the pain of returning his two young sons to their mother's home on Sunday nights. But, he remarked to me, "I thought a guy who didn't pay child support didn't give a damn about his kids, but that's not always the case. I used to think those guys who never saw their kids were bastards. I never thought I'd hear myself say that those guys get a bum rap. But taking my kids back on Sunday nights put me through torture. It hurt so much that I came close to skipping town. Men have trouble feeling these things, and they deal by running away."

Glenn did not run away, but one evening he threw albums filled with his children's photos into a coal stove as a way of trying to obliterate his pain. He had so many built-up resentments that he needed a purgative outlet. Until then, Glenn was not receptive to direct counseling, but now he feared he was "crazy," and knew he had to draw on his grief in a more constructive way. He began therapy and decided that he was too hurt and angry to keep living and working in the same city as his family. He moved from Connecticut to another state, but talked to his sons daily by telephone. For him, two weeks in the summer and Christmas vacation was better than having to leave them on Sunday nights. When his sons became teenagers, however, they chose to live with him.

Men struggle with the effort of trying to be good fathers after separation and divorce. Even men who were not used to having time alone with their children prior to the divorce, still feel loss. In the opinion of Irene Surmik, a social worker with Families in Transition, "Separation and divorce raise questions for men about what it means to be a father and how to perform that role when they are no longer under the same roof. If he's a noncustodial parent, he's always saying hello and good-bye. He's constantly coping with loss, both the child's and his own. This is very hard for men who have been socialized—not to deal with feelings. They come to this experience with much less skill than women. Sometimes men deal with grief by cutting their losses and moving on. They struggle with whether they are important to the child other than as a breadwinner. They question whether the child really needs or misses them."

The emotional burden of divorced men who care about their children is generally unrecognized. They fear being left out in the cold. They see child custody as mysterious, and worry that they have little or no right to gain primary physical custody of their children or even an acceptable partial custody schedule.

The current standard guiding the courts in custody cases emphasizes the overall emotional best interest and welfare of the child. Neither parent is presumed to be better suited for that responsibility. Attorneys, judges, psychologists, and social workers agree that divorced fathers, for the most part, want to have more involvement in their children's lives than they did even ten years ago. In 1974, Dr. Haim Ginott, in his bestselling book *Between Parent and Child*, warned that if a father becomes too involved with the ordinary tasks of child care, "the baby may end up with two mothers, rather than a mother and a father." But now fathers are routinely in the delivery room, participating in the birth of their children, cutting the umbilical cord. From the beginning, they are encouraged to be more nurturing.

In earlier times, when wives and children were considered to be property, husbands had custody of the children. In this century, most jurisdictions applied the "Tender Years Doctrine," thinking that young children were better off living with their mothers. In most cases today, divorcing parents decide on their own custody arrangements. When disputes occur, however, the trend since the late seventies is for courts to be more gender-neutral in determining what is in the overall emotional best interest of the child. The playing field has leveled significantly since the mid-seventies, when no state allowed joint custody of children in divorce cases.

Court Standards for Custody

When parents cannot work out a mutually acceptable arrangement for custody, the court intervenes, applying the "best interest" standard. In cases of conflict, the court in every instance must determine which parent has primary physical custody of the children, and then establish a partial custody schedule for the other parent. The standard partial custody arrangement is every other weekend from Friday after school until Sunday evening, plus one evening a week for dinner.

The court also has to consider the possibility of shared custody, meaning that a child's time is equally divided between the homes of both parents, who have equal responsibility for the child's care, including decisions affecting religious training, education, and medical attention. When custody is contested by either parent, the court requires the testimony of court-appointed experts to contribute an unbiased opinion, based upon their study of the family. In increasing numbers, the courts are awarding joint legal custody. Children divide their time between both parents, or live with one parent, but both mother and father share equally in decisions. For example, in California, joint legal custody is established in 80 percent of all divorces.

One Foot in the Bucket

While divorcing parents are well advised to keep abreast of the latest rulings in their states, gender biases are waning in the courts with respect to the child-care capabilities of either parent. "But because the law no longer assumes that one parent is better suited than another to raise the kids doesn't mean that society or men have changed their consciousness," pointed out Neil Rosenblum, Ph.D., a clinical psychologist specializing in custody evaluations throughout western Pennsylvania. "From my experience, men going through a divorce presume that custody of the children will automatically go to the wife, and they haven't a chance. That isn't so, but men do have one foot in the bucket. They are a step behind the eight ball when it comes time to take a look at custody in the courts."

Men have one foot in the bucket because to determine the overall best emotional interest of the child, the court is concerned with the bonding that exists between the child and parent. Regardless of the fact that men are redefining their roles as fathers, a father's day-to-day involvement in the lives of his children seldom corresponds to the time commitment the average mother gives to child-care responsibilities, even when she works outside the home. In the eyes of the court, a father has to earn his right to custody by demonstrating his ability, for example, to get children up and out for school, pack their lunches, prepare their dinner, help with schoolwork, give baths, and put them to bed. Mothers rather than fathers are more generally responsible for these bonding rituals. "So while courts say that discrimination doesn't exist and the tender years doctrine is gone," maintained Rosenblum, "the philosophy still remains, 'If it ain't broke, don't fix it.'"

Judge Lawrence W. Kaplan, past president of the Association of Family and Conciliation Courts, points the finger directly at judges and the system that appoints or elects them. "In more enlightened jurisdictions," he told me, "fathers do not come up against the residual thinking of the tender years law. But many judges hold on to the sympathetic prejudice that mothers are more nurturing, and fathers should be sidelined to the weekends."

This attitude is less likely to exist in jurisdictions where judges are elected or appointed to family courts, and specialize in the issues of marriage, family life, and divorce. "Men get a fairer shake when judges are informed in family law and take their obligations seriously," Kaplan continued. "But when judges move from court to court, or hear all types of cases in a rural setting, their understanding of family law can be limited. It's especially unfortunate when custody cases, for example, are part of the civil docket and are heard with other civil cases, between fender benders and malpractice suits. Many judges don't like this aspect of family law, and do it by the seat of their pants. So horror stories do exist."

Activist Fathers' Groups

To eliminate the horror stories, activist groups are springing up across the United States trying to advance the cause of fathers' rights. Among them in the Boston area, for example, are Citizens for Divorce Equality, Dads Against Divorce Discrimination (DADD), and Concerned Fathers of Massachusetts. The absence of a group in a particular geographic area usually indicates that issues affecting fathers are underrepresented, and men are probably uninformed about the importance of their role in their children's development.

Bruce Burrows, spokesman for Fathers United for Equal Rights in the Potomac-Chesapeake area (one of the nation's oldest advocacy groups founded in 1976), used a sports analogy to describe the naive understanding fathers have regarding their custody rights. "Men approach the issue like a sports game, where the referees make the decisions. If they play by the rules, men think they have a fair chance of winning. But that's not true. Judges are not referees, and the rules are stacked against them. We have predominately male judges. Where do older men get their notions of what is good for children, that they rule against men? I'd like to ask why they think it's better for children to be with their mother rather than with someone like themselves."

The philosophy, "If it ain't broke, don't fix it," does prevail in most family courts. Whoever has had temporary custody, unless the arrangement proves not to be in the overall best interest of the child, will generally gain primary physical custody after divorce. A woman is favored by this thinking because evidence indicates that she is usually the primary custodial parent during separation. Therefore, a mother's involvement in the daily routine of diapering, bathing, feeding, and chauffeuring usually means that it is her care that will continue to provide for the best overall emotional interest of the child.

Once husband and wife are separated, a standard arrangement has the father visiting his children every other weekend, one night for dinner on the off week, some holidays, and two to four weeks during the summer. This agreement is then made permanent by the courts after the divorce.

"It's Where You Start"

If a father wants more involvement in the day-to-day life of his child, the best strategy, according to lawyers, psychologists, and social workers, is for him to be an integral part of the child's life before the divorce occurs. They advocate that a father wanting more than traditional custody arrangements should not leave the family home until he has a legal agreement with his wife that is acceptable to him regarding their relationship with the children. In the worst cases, a father will disappear during separation or stay away from the children because of the hostility between him and his wife, or due to his own depression.

However, specialists contend that in the interim between separation and divorce, fathers should try to see their children more, not less, and strive to maintain as much contact as possible. Some fathers assume that the courts will not permit them to have shared custody, or think that at some future time they will return to court to negotiate an arrangement that they will like better. In reality, a father who has been absent from his child's life has little hope that the court will change his custody arrangement based only on his promises. What goes around, comes around. The less involved he has been with the child, the less his chances. The more involved, the better his chances.

The strongest advantage either parent can have with respect to gaining custody is, then, to have custody during separation. Attorney Norma Chase made the point very clear: "Some parts of the country are more enlightened than others regarding custody, but today I think *Kramer vs. Kramer* would have been decided differently in most courts. Decisions are not as automatic as they once were in favor of the mother. But a father cannot sit on his rights and make grand plans for custody at some future time when he is not doing anything to maintain his relationship with kids in the interim because he can't stand his wife or his wife's boyfriend. If he cares about his kids, he has to put up with her because it's in the best interest of his kids for him to see them."

To underscore the point that fathers ought to negotiate a legal separation before moving from the family home, Neil Rosenblum suggested that two fathers can be identical in the quality of their relationship with their children. But the father who had temporary shared custody during separation will fare better in a court decision. "For the courts," Rosenblum said, "it's where you start. If a father leaves and assumes that his wife is going to be generous and liberal with visitation and not keep him from the kids—don't be surprised. Some women will. Therefore, if a father's goal is shared custody or primary custody, his chances are not very high if he leaves home without a temporary agreement. The primary custodial parent has to practically self-destruct. That's why men in fathers' rights groups who are angry with the courts don't feel that they are treated fairly. It's not the court's fault, but part of a more complex societal issue. Fathers need to be educated about custody in their jurisdiction, and from day one they have to be involved with their children."

A temporary custodial agreement, drawn by an attorney specializing in family law, will clearly state when a mother and father will be with their children. A man truly wanting to be involved with his children's daily routine will make sure that the agreement will steer away from the weekend father syndrome. He will specify overnight options that include school nights. Furthermore, he will live within easy commuting distance so that the children are able to maintain their school and church affiliations. When a father is a father in the complete sense of the word, he has an equal chance for primary or shared physical custody. Parents who negotiate such arrangements for the overall emotional best interest of their children create a new status quo, and the courts will be inclined to agree that it should be permanent. A father who mediates his terms before divorce and follows through with his commitment is less likely to hear the question, "But where were you when the kids needed you?" or "Where were you, Dad, when I was growing up?"

Modifying Custody Arrangements

Custody is always ruled on before the court and can be modified at any time upon a showing of changed circumstances. In effect, no arrangement is permanent, but it is a heavy burden to change an existing custody arrangement unless a serious complaint exists about the fitness of the other person. A father cannot move out of his home, get himself situated, and then say he wants the children. The husband who takes a walk or has been a Sunday-afternoon-at-the-park father cannot expect the court to listen when he shouts his own praises in the courtroom, wanting to increase his custody time.

An experienced attorney in the practice of family law, bluntly translated: "Men have to earn their right to custody or shared custody. There's no free lunch. Men have to prove that they can be nurturers. It's more than simply ballyhooing, 'I want custody,' and offering promises. That's a big-boy, sophomoric attitude. Are they willing to take children to school, entertain them on the floor playing 'Chutes and Ladders'? Will they check homework, be home for dinner? Can they buy a daughter her first bra? Mothers have been buying their sons jockstraps for years. Once fathers can do a lot of these things, then they can make a run for the roses. If they can't, then they are kidding themselves about custody or shared custody. Custody isn't on-the-job training. It's not a matter of saying, 'I want.' That's all hype. The pivotal point on which the courts decide is the overall emotional best interest of the child."

The Right Attorney

For the courts, the rule of thumb in child custody is "where you start." Ideally, husbands need to be involved fathers from the day of their children's birth. If they want shared physical custody or frequent opportunities to be with their children, then they need to finalize an agreement before officially separating. To plan ahead, fathers should engage attorneys specializing in family law. Men often err by retaining the same lawyers advising them on real estate or income tax. Feeling comfortable with an attorney who is an old confidant on the golf course or at the Rotary Club is no substitute for the expertise of an attorney whose primary practice is divorce.

The need for female validation may also influence a man's choice of an attorney. Men beginning divorce proceedings sometimes believe that a woman attorney will be more sensitive to their emotional needs. But divorce attorneys concur that the best place for clients to deal with emotional trauma is in the offices of psychologists or psychiatrists, not in law firms. Attorneys specializing in family law are generally aware that divorce is a personal crisis and advise their clients to seek psychological support.

Some men also think that their wives will be more upset to see them represented by a woman. Attorney Joanne Ross-Wilder, past chair of the Family Division of Lawyers of the Pennsylvania Bar Association, noted, "If a man comes into my office expecting that I will understand his wife and therefore cause her more anxiety, I tell him clearly that his premise is invalid. To start an important lawyer-client relationship on that premise is only going to lead to problems. That assumption gets in the way of understanding the legal process and the goals that should be attained."

A more cynical observation by women attorneys notes the simplicity of men who think that female representation will influence a judge to consider, "If a woman took him on, he can't be all that bad." Nonetheless, attorney Hilary Spatz, who represents more men than women in divorce cases, told me that she is convinced that "there are a lot of *mensches* out there. Men who want to know about their responsibilities to their families and how to live up to them don't get enough good press. But they shouldn't calculate that a woman lawyer will be another weapon in their arsenal."

Competence and shared values, rather than gender, should be the basis for choosing a divorce attorney, agree men and women practicing family law. "Maybe it's not that important if you like your patent attorney," Ross-Wilder remarked further, "but a chemistry has to exist between a lawyer and a client who wants a divorce. If a man wants custody of his children, for example, he should not be represented by a lawyer, whether male or female, who has only a traditional understanding of the family structure."

A father wanting to negotiate favorable custody arrangements must therefore begin with sound legal advice. Before complaining that the court system is against him, a man needs to consider how well prepared he is to assume the custody arrangement that he wants. Equally important, he needs to retain a lawyer who can give him the proper representation to prove it. To avoid the name-calling of contested custody cases, some lawyers prefer that the divorcing parents themselves determine their custody with the help of qualified professionals, such as social workers or psychologists. Nonetheless, the special attention of legal counsel is required in the preparation of the case.

Advantages of Mediation

The Association of Family and Conciliation Courts, an international association of judges, counselors, court evaluators, mediators, and lawyers concerned about marriage and family life, recommends that mediation is helpful for couples wanting to arrive at solutions regarding the emotional best interest of their children, both before and after divorce. Mediators are neutral professionals educated in family law and psychology, and skilled in negotiation techniques. The Association clarifies that mediation is not marital counseling, but focuses on helping parents to reach agreements "so that parents and children may better adjust to the divorce and resolve future issues together."

Mediation is not a substitute for legal advice; lawyers write up final agreements. But mediators can help couples narrow the issues and limit the time and expense of going to court, if some matters can be settled without a lawyer's time and court costs. Husbands particularly prefer mediation when angry wives threaten to obstruct their relationship with their children. In fact, mediation services are provided by most courts to help couples resolve custody and visitation disputes. In some jurisdictions, mediation is required by law or court rule when such disagreement persists. Professional mediators are available for private service and are listed in the telephone directory yellow pages. Family services connected with the courts can offer advice regarding mediation services available in the community.

Psychologists and social workers who do custody evaluations for the court maintain that they can quickly distinguish between men legitimately wanting to be more involved with their children and those pursuing custody in order to seek revenge; punish their wives; or extend their power, authority, and control. But, forced to face the choice between becoming an involved father or losing that role completely, men often become better fathers as a result of divorce. Clinical examples and daily experience reveal men who have become more loving with their children and have successfully proceeded through the court system to gain extended custody.

"Sometimes I wish an ex-wife could be a bug on the wall to see how her ex-husband has grown in a relationship with their children," clinical psychologist Neil Rosenblum observed. "I often encourage divorced parents to spend time together with a child so that the mother can see the fine parent her ex-husband has become. If this were always possible, I think a lot of litigation could be avoided, possibly the divorce. I've heard women say, 'If I knew he could have been such a good parent, I might not have divorced him. We might have had a shot.' But I can't blame the woman for being angry because she's operating on what the guy was like years ago. If he sat on his duff drinking beer and watching ballgames, and he now takes little Susie to ballet, it's hard for her to fathom. And sometimes that happens."

Nonetheless, many fathers who have the will to relate to their children may not know how. Although they seldom slip through the custody evaluation process of the court, there are husbands who will wage costly battles for extended visitation only to deposit their children at the home of their own parents for care and entertainment. From her experience as a counselor to families in transition, Irene Surmik offered the observation that "fathers often feel that lots of events have to be planned. I try to have them understand that simple things are more important, like having breakfast together, or planning lunch, or playing board games. It's in the caretaking of children that relationships are forged. Fathers often think that mothers have some magical ways or innate knowledge of how to do this. But mothers learn through day-to-day interaction. When fathers understand that mothers learn by trial and error, then the mystique of child care is removed, and they feel that they can learn to do the same."

As a result of separation and divorce, fathers often think more seriously about what it means to be a father and invest more creative energy in relating to their children. It is not unusual for them to build stronger emotional ties than if they had remained in a traditional family structure where father is breadwinner and disciplinarian, and mother is chief caretaker. In a dual-career marriage where husbands and wives strive to divide domestic labor, mother still assumes the lion's share of child care, and father is her reliable pinchhitter.

In her book, *The Second Shift*, sociologist Arlie Hochschild estimated that only about 20 percent of fathers are fully involved with the chores of parenting. "Most women work one shift at the office or factory and a 'second shift' at home," concluded Hochschild.

After divorcing, ex-husbands frequently discover new capacities in themselves for being more involved dads. For example, fathers who were marginal parents during tense marriages often become more devoted after divorce. Consequently, some divorced couples are more likely to communicate better with respect to their children than they did while married. They will cover for each other in emergencies, make sure they live within walking distance of each other, and coordinate flexible vacations. But when a devoted father feels handicapped in his efforts to maintain a spontaneous relationship with his children because life does not run on tight weekend scheduling, he has to proceed through expensive litigation in order to change his visitation arrangements. Meanwhile, his ex-wife, who once carried the major burden of child care, is often loath to forget that a divorce contributed to the revolution in his behavior.

Ideally, fathers could avoid expense and psychological turmoil by forging a close relationship with their children from the day of birth. If divorce is inevitable, then a wise mother recognizes that for the children's overall emotional best interest, involvement with their father should not only be maintained, but encouraged. When parents are able to surrender their gauntlets and agree on a legal custody arrangement before separating—either through mediation, counseling, or by themselves—the court will generally honor their decision, and legal fees will not escalate.

The favored position is that both divorced parents are positively involved with their children. "The best parent is both parents," is the current thinking. "Even though there are times when separating parents wish that the other would drop off the face of the earth, they are the only two people who have a natural and rational bond with the children they have produced," remarked counselor Irene Surmik. "It's ultimately better for the child if parents in transition can look ahead and put their parenting and divorcing into perspective. At the time of separation, feelings are high. But that doesn't mean that things can't get better down the road. What doesn't seem possible now for separating parents to agree about regarding the children, can be possible later."

Divorcing parents can become very discouraged, however, in their efforts to try to end their marital relationship while continuing their parenting. In order to help parents during this stressful time, counselors highly recommend *Mom's House, Dad's House: Making Shared Custody Work,* by Isolina Ricci, Ph.D. More recent books are *Daddy's Home*, by Mike Clary; *Parent vs. Parent: How You and Your Child Can Survive the Custody Battle*, by Dr. Stephen Herman; *Second Chances: Men, Women, and Children a Decade After Divorce*, by Judith S. Wallerstein & Sandra Blakeslee; and *The Nurturing Father*, by Dr. Kyle D. Pruett.

Chris Stafford began *Full-Time Dads*, a journal for fathers, when he and his wife decided that he would stay home and take care of their children. Realizing the lack of material directed toward men in parenting magazines, he started his own. *Full-Time Dads* "features material of, by, and for its members to establish open communication and a free exchange of ideas and information that encourage support, discussion, growth, fellowship, and resource sharing." Letters to the editor indicate how full-time, divorced, and separated fathers value this unpretentious journal.

Also highly recommended is *Speak Out for Children*, the quarterly newsletter of The National Council for Children's Rights (NCCR), in Washington, D.C. All of the publications, conferences, and efforts of NCCR "are concerned with the healthy development of children of divorced and separated parents [by] minimizing hostilities between parents who are involved in marital disputes, substituting conciliation and mediation for the adversarial approach, assuring a child's access to both parents, and providing equitable child support."

Children adjust better to divorce if parents minimize the conflict between them regarding arrangements for the children, and respect each other. The trend of the courts is to facilitate this transition by recognizing the important role of fathers in childrearing. Yet, men will berate the court system and say, "I was a good father," solely on the basis of being a successful and steady breadwinner, providing for a child's economic welfare while overlooking opportunities for emotional involvement.

The court is not, however, the real or only culprit for estranging a father from his children. The problem is also personal and societal. Ideally, men can rescue themselves from the impasse of anger and disillusionment with the legal system by participating actively in the total lives of their children from the moment of birth. Furthermore, they need to be aware of current thinking among children's advocates claiming that children after divorce are better off if both parents preserve their parenting role. In itself, divorce does not mean that a father or mother is, by necessity, alienated from the children. But myths from old laws hover in courtrooms, and also cling to the consciousness of fathers who do not think they have a chance to participate equally in a child's upbringing after divorce.

Men often maintain a stubborn resistance to listening to the best advice, and embrace as truth anecdotal evidence passed on third-hand about a disenfranchised husband of another time and place. No doubt horror stories exist, but nightmares are less frequent for fathers who choose legal counsel that is current on family law to inform them about custodial rights in their jurisdiction, negotiate temporary custody arrangements before leaving the home, and maintain strong relationships with their children before and after separation.

THE LOCKER ROOM

Here I am in the locker room with my friend David . . .
   "Have you ever had a locker-room conversa-tion about women—you know, the way women think we do, talking in explicit detail about what we did with our dates the night before?"
   "No, I said. I never have."
   "You know why women think we have these ex-plicit conversations? Because they do, that's why. Women talk about everything."

from *Travels*, by Michael Crichton

MEN AND WOMEN WHO live in the same world, neighborhood, and house still assume that they are basically very different. A gender war is even said to be raging. The "Locker Room" and the "Women's Room" are contemporary symbols that reflect our accepted images of how the other sex really looks and acts. Anyone trespassing into de-fined male or female space becomes the mysterious "Other," com-pelled to struggle for identification in territory where men and women have clear ideas about how the other best fits in.

Women have long known the pressure of conforming to guidelines guaranteeing that their presence will go unnoticed. My interviews with ex-husbands suggest that men also suffer the confinement of keeping to their place, and want to move beyond behavior that defines and limits them. The difference is that men seldom initiate change until personal tragedy or the vagaries of life force them to do so. Men usually just stumble into the Women's Room, and when they do, women can hardly believe their eyes.

Men who feel the pain of divorce express a perplexing need to experience growth and acceptance. The confidence that stems from financial security and personal charm does not relieve these instincts. A handsome and successful man, 45 years old, describing his adjustment to the singles scene, found little joy in life since his wife of ten years left: "I never knew what rebound meant, but I find I can't hurt another woman or treat her casually because I now relate to her. I don't know if I ever looked at a woman like that. I respect the emotions of women. I don't think I could ever say that up until now."

When the circumstances of divorce compel men to wander a while through unknown rooms and feel in their gut what it is like to be the "Other" or the "Second Sex," they develop a new consciousness about themselves and their interpersonal relationships. They are more expressive about interpreting and sharing their inner lives. Their words belie the persistent stereotype that men are hostile, resistant, or, at best, indifferent to evaluating prescribed masculine attitudes.

"I'm going through emotions and sensitivities that I would have considered to be feminizing 20 years ago," admitted a former U.S. Army colonel, one year after his divorce. "I know emotions can hurt because I'm bonkers from this divorce. I respect the emotions of women and that they have been hurt in a way I never thought possible. My ex-wife says that I'll probably make a wonderful mate for another woman. And I say, 'What about us?' But she says it's too late."

The detractions against women in the last decade that Susan Faludi brilliantly analyzes in *Backlash: The Undeclared War Against American Women* have backfired on the American man. The effort to advance the message that the freedoms of feminism have contributed to the unhappiness of the American woman and the rise of divorce, has promoted the false assumption that divorce is an emotional trauma for women, but not for men. When ex-husbands want their turn to say that their experience is also devastating, the success of backlash—the creation of a male culture, whether the individual architects are men or women—causes their credibility to be challenged and their voices to be muffled.

And so we find it a strain to believe men who say that divorce has made them more appreciative of the simple pleasures of family life, more aware of imposed definitions of maleness, and more tuned-in to the feelings of their former wives. Jerry Fusione is a representative example.

He explained, "My wife and I really can't be friends, but we have to cooperate for the sake of the children, who shouldn't always have to deal with a hassle. Peggy sat next to me at our son's high school play. I even felt sorry for her when Keith walked away with me. I knew that hurt her because I understand how it feels to be excluded from the family."

Women, more than men, have for centuries experienced the role of Outsider. To hear a man identify his feelings with a woman's is a new experience. But backlash would have us believe that only women suffer empathetic insights, whereas men are blind to the feelings of others in their desire to preserve their traditional roles and maintain the status quo.

Another example of an ex-husband comfortable with changing gender roles is Tony Barnes, who won primary custody of his two teenaged daughters when his wife left to live with another man. "The house brought the girls back to me. They wanted to be in the same school. I had the dog, their beds, their rooms. I'm at home with their stuffed animals and luggage. Who would believe it? When the girls return to college after vacations, it's terrible for me. Until I get my own beat again, I hate an empty house."

Women have always written in their journals about the silence of a house once the children leave. To hear a man make the same remark is unexpected. The code of the Locker Room appears to be violated. A favorite belief is that divorced men yearn to escape into its restorative comfort. But many of the men I interviewed seemed willing to jockey for another place.

From their own suffering, many divorced men become more responsive to the feelings of others. They begin to place more value on their relationships, bringing into balance their commitment to career or business. The ironic denouement is that a second wife often reaps the benefit of an ex-husband's willingness to reflect on his vulnerabilities. From the light of the first marriage, he thinks more openly about the dynamics of an emotional relationship with a woman. He lets down his defenses and softens the edges of rigid masculine conduct. This is a painful transition for many men.

Gene Baker, an urban policy expert, swiveled in his chair and gazed beyond the skyline. "The pain that I feel is really overwhelming at times," he reflected. "I hope the worst is behind me. I look back at what I was, and know I was abusive in many respects. I was authoritarian and autocratic. But that's the way I was raised. I'd do a lot of things differently in another marriage, a lot of things better knowing what I now know. First of all, I'd be more responsible and careful about being compatible. I'd listen better, talk and listen. My ideals of commitment and fidelity haven't changed, but my attitudes have about intimacy and a kind of day-to-day style."

In general, hurt men are often willing to be introspective to the point of adjusting their priorities. But the unquestioned assumption that men want to live for competition, work, and success undercuts trust in their efforts. Throughout history, men have exercised authority over every aspect of women's lives. Both men and women are, therefore, tempted to be wary when former husbands question traditional male behavior or relate their own accounts of feeling demeaned, degraded, and victimized.

Their stories being neither solicited nor trusted, divorced men are allowed off the hook. For some, this is the benefit of backlash. They are exempted from the personal and societal obligation of figuring out why their marriages did not last. That leaves the burden of deciding how men best act as husbands and fathers to the testimony of women. Yet ex-husbands and ex-wives might better spend their time reshaping themselves, not each other. The more self-awareness a man gains through separation and divorce, the less likely he is to be stoically silent about how divorce affects him. Therefore, men can be as responsible for their self-definition as husbands and fathers, as women are for their roles as wives and mothers.

For too long, women, as well as men, have imagined too little about each other's capacities. Indeed, both sexes have used the other for selfish ends. No one knows this better than couples who have divorced. Yet the primary discussion on divorce (at least up until now) has accumulated its meaning from the experiences of women. Even though men make up one-half of each union, their words are not always heeded. Ultimately, men should be as accountable for voicing their experience of marriage and divorce as women are. For, only men can express what separation and divorce puts them through.

To tell the stories of divorced men is not to redress the balance by placing them in a futile struggle against the words of divorced women. But as long as the subject of divorce remains a woman's monologue, the conversation is stuck. The Locker Room and the Women's Room will continue to remain mysteries to each other, when, in fact, their territory is much the same. We need to see that both men and women endure emotional exploitation, incompatibility, and abusive behavior. Both husbands and wives know the tension of balancing family and career. The stories of ex-husbands have their own share of heartbreak.

Personal stories are the best ways we have of understanding how men and women live, think, and feel, regardless of pervading theories and ideologies. They have the power to expose life as it goes on around us. They give breadth to abstract conflicts. They speak more powerfully than statistics. They reveal issues deserving of further research.

The accounts of former husbands allow men and women to enter more places than we know of on a strictly personal basis. As we become more knowledgeable in these areas, the plots of divorce become more familiar, but less conventional. Contradictory to rumors of war, we see that the genders are not polar opposites. Similar problems, both public and private, press in on them. The stories of divorced men can, as a result, deepen the rapport that men and women share, to the point of revealing even in the contradictions of divorce, the inseparable bonds of human nature.

Ideally, the stories in *Men On Divorce* serve as mirrors for men who are newly divorced or separated, or for husbands and wives who suffer in troubled marriages, allowing them to see themselves better, empathize with each other to a greater extent, and eventually heal.

APPENDIX

National Organizations

These organizations will generally provide material and newsletters, or information regarding programs or support groups in various cities.

American Association of Marriage and Family Therapists
1717 K Street, N.W.
Washington, D.C. 22036

Association of Family and Conciliation Courts
329 W. Wilson Street
Madison, WI 53703
(608) 251-4001

Children's Defense Fund
122 G Street, N.W.
Washington, D.C. 20001
(202) 628-8787

F.A.I.R.
The National Father's Organization
1 N.E. 10th Street
Milford, DE 19963
(302) 422-8460

Joint Custody Association
10606 Wilkins Avenue
Los Angeles, CA 90024
(213) 474-4859

National Child Support Advocacy Coalition
6818 Rock Creek Court
Alexandria, VA 22306
(703) 765-7956

National Congress for Men and Children
2020 Pennsylvania Avenue
Washington, D.C. 20003
(202) 328-4277

The National Council for Children's Rights
220 I Street, N.E.
Washington, D.C. 20002
(202) 547-6227

OMEGA
Institute for Holistic Studies
260 Lake Drive
Rhinebeck, NY 12572-3212

Stepfamily Association of America, Inc.
215 Centennial Hall, S.
Lincoln, NE 68508
(402) 477-7837

Therapeutic Touch
Nurse Healers-Professional Associates, Inc.
175 Fifth Aveneue, Suite 2755
New York, NY 10010

A Sample of Men's Councils and Collectives

The Austin Men's Center
1611 West Sixth Street
Austin, TX 78703
(512) 477-9595

Colorado Men's Council
P.O. Box 4795
Boulder, CO 80306
(305) 444-7797

Indiana Men's Council
4611 Broadway
Indianapolis, IN 46205

The Men's Center of Los Angeles
9012 Burton Way
Beverly Hills, CA 90221
(818) 701-9898

The Men's Center of St. Louis
7700 Clayton Road
St. Louis, MO 63117

The Men's Council of Washington
7750 16th Street, N.W.
Washington, D.C. 20012
(703) 820-9097

On the Common Ground
A Center for Men in New York City
250 West 57th Street
Suite 1527
New York, NY 10107
(212) 265-0584

Pittsburgh Men's Collective
5860 Forward Avenue
Pittsburgh, PA 15217
(412) 421-6405

Seattle M.E.N.
Men's Evolvement Network
602 W. Howe Street
Seattle, WA 98119

Texas Men's Center
8012 Shin Oak Drive
San Antonio, TX 78233
(512) 945-9112

Twin Cities Men's Center
3255 Hennepin Avenue, South
Minneapolis, MN 55408
(612) 822-5892

Directories, Journals, Newsletters, Magazines

The Chesapeake Men's Exchange
60 South Aberdeen Street
Arlington, VA 22204

The Drum: A Newsletter of the Washington Men's Council
214 Belvedere Blvd., #6
Silver Spring, MD 20902

Full-Time Dads: A Journal for Fathers
Chris Stafford, Publisher/Editor
P.O. Box 120773
St. Paul, MN 55112-0773
(612) 633-7424

Guide to Greater New York Men's Groups and Events
New Views Educational Services
P.O. Box 137
Little Ferry, NJ 07643

International Parenting Directory of Organizations
The National Council for Children's Rights
220 I Street, N.E., Suite 230
Washington, D.C. 20002

MAN!
1611 W. Sixth Street
Austin TX 78703
(512) 474-6401

Men's Council Journal
Boulder Men's Council
Box 4795
Boulder, CO 80306

Men's Resource Directory
788 Reservoir Avenue
Cranston, RI 02910

Men's Resource Hotline
Gordon Clay, ed.
P.O. Box 882-WS
San Anselmo, CA 94979-0882
(415) 453-2839

Men Talk
Twin Cities Men's Center
3255 South Hennepin Avenue
Minneapolis, MN 55408
(612) 822-5892

Speak Out for Children
The National Council for Children's Rights, Inc.
220 I Street, N.E.
Suite 230
Washington, D.C. 20002-4362

The Talking Stick: A Newsletter About Men
Dr. Bruce Barth, ed.
182 Thomas Jefferson Drive
Frederick, MD 21701
(301) 829-21701

Thunder Stick
3392 West 34th Avenue
Vancouver, BC V6N 2K6
(604) 290-9988

Wingspan: Journal of the Male Spirit
Dick Halloran, publisher
Box 23550
Brightmoor Station
Detroit, MI 48223
(313) 273-4330

Baraff, Alvin. *Men Talk: How Men Really Feel About Women; Sex, Relationships and Themselves*. New York: E.P. Dutton, 1992.

Beauvoir, Simone de. *The Second Sex*. Translated by H.M. Parshley. New York: Knopf, 1957.

Bly Robert. *Iron John: A Book About Men*. New York: Addison-Wesley, 1990.

Clary, Mike. *Daddy's Home*. New York: The Talman Co., Inc., 1991.

Erkel, R. Todd. "A New Man." *Pitt Magazine*. September, 1989, 30–35.

Faludi, Susan. *Backlash: The Undeclared War Against the American Woman*. New York: Crown Publishers, Inc., 1991.

French, Marilyn. *The Women's Room*. New York: Summit Books, 1977.

Friedan, Betty. *The Feminine Mystique*. New York: Dell, 1963.

Gilligan, Carol. *In A Different Voice: Psychological Theory and Women's Development*. Cambridge, MA.: Harvard University Press, 1982.

Herman, Dr. Stephen. *Parent vs Parent: How You and Your Child Can Survive the Custody Battle*. New York: Pantheon, 1990.

Hochschild, Arlie. *The Second Shift: Working Parents and the Revolution at Home*. New York: Viking, 1989.

Jong, Erica. *Fear of Flying*. New York: Holt, Rinehart & Winston, 1973.

Keen, Sam. *Fire in the Belly: On Being a Man*. New York: Bantam, 1991.

Kübler-Ross, Elisabeth, M.D. *On Death and Dying*. New York: Macmillan Publishing Company, 1966.

Lewin, Carl. *The Heritage of Illusions*. St. Louis, MO: Warren H. Green, Inc., 1977.

Miller, Stuart. *Men and Friendship*. Los Angeles, CA: Jeremy P. Tarcher, 1992.

Moore, Robert and Douglas Gillette. *King, Warrior, Magician, Lover: Rediscovering the Archetypes of the Mature Masculine*. San Francisco, CA: Harper, 1990.

Myers, Michael F. *Men and Divorce*. New York: The Guilford Press, 1989.

O'Connor, Terrance. "A Day for Men." *Networker*. May/June, 1990, 36–39.

Peck, M. Scott, M.D. *The Road Less Traveled: A New Psychology of Love, Traditional Values and Spiritual Growth*. New York: A Touchstone Book, 1978.

Pruett, Dr. Kyle D. *The Nurturing Father*. New York: Warner Books, 1988.

Ricci, Isolina, Ph.D. *Mom's House, Dad's House: Making Shared Custody Work*. New York: Collier Books, 1990.

Rubin, Lillian B. *Intimate Strangers*. New York: Harper & Row, 1983.

Strauss, Murray A. and Richard Gelles. *Physical Violence in American Families*. New Brunswick, NJ: Transaction Publishers, 1990.

Tannen, Deborah, Ph.D. *You Just Don't Understand*. New York: Ballantine Books, 1990.

Trafford, Abigail. *Crazy Time: Surviving Divorce*. New York: Harper & Row, 1982.

Thompson, Keith, ed. *To Be A Man: In Search of the Deep Masculine*. Los Angeles, CA: Jeremy P. Tarcher, 1991.

Wallerstein, Judith S. and Sandra Blakeslee. *Second Chances: Men, Women, and Children A Decade After Divorce*. New York: Ticknor & Fields, 1990.

Wolf, Naomi. *Fire With Fire: The New Female Power and How It Will Change the 21st Century*. New York: Random House, 1993.

Wymard, Ellie, Ph.D. *Divorced Women, New Lives: Encouraging Words and Realistic Advice From Ex-Wives Who Understand*. New York: Ballantine Books, 1990.

Ellie Wymard, Ph.D., the author of *Divorced Women, New Lives,* is a professor of English at Carlow College in Pittsburgh, Pennsylvania, where she developed and taught some of the first courses on women in the country. Her critical essays have appeared in scholarly journals, and she continues to publish a series of interviews with nationally recognized women writers in *The Critic.* She has also appeared on national television and radio programs.

Dr. Wymard lives both in Pittsburgh, and in Chatham, Massachusetts, with her husband, Joseph, an attorney. They have two adult sons.

We hope you enjoyed this Hay House book.
If you would like to receive a free catalog featuring additional
Hay House books and products, or if you would like information
about the Hay Foundation, please write to:

Hay House, Inc.
1154 E. Dominguez St.
P.O. Box 6204
Carson, CA 90749-6204

or call:

(800) 654-5126